for 13 Teaching Solutions

	7 PROMPT ASSIGNMENTS	8 OPEN ESSAY	9 CUBING	10 KILLER THESIS: THREE-IN-ONE	11 BOO... REPORT ESSAYS	...AREAS	...G ...UR... ...ES FROM GREAT PIECES
Activity							
Teaching Solutions	If you want them to respond to a prompt for fast habit development	If you want them to make all of the choices	If you want them to focus on developing a body of informational content	If you want them to develop a thesis first	If you want them to write an essay about a book they've read (or any literature)	If you want them to use these skills for other content	If you want them to use the moves of other writers
Basic Steps	1. Assignment prompt and three to five structures 2. Kernel essay (write/share) 3. Flesh out with details	1. Students write truism/thesis 2. Choose structure from all choices 3. Kernel essay (write/share) 4. Flesh out with details	1. Cubing infoshots 2. Follow-up assignment for polish 3. Retrace steps by keeping/putting infoshot templates into writer's notebooks or journals	1. Develop truism 2. Cast truism into a three-in-one 3. Identify the parts of this new thesis 4. Write about each part to flesh it out	1. Read book 2. Choose aspect of book 3. Choose structure 4. Write/share kernel essay 5. Flesh out kernel into a detailed essay	1. Figure out structures to match required piece 2. Try out those structures as kernels 3. Flesh out if required for situation	1. Read a piece 2. Chunk it 3. Summarize each chunk 4. Cast into text structure 5. Try out the structure with other content
Tools	Text structure choices; expository prompts; kernel essay planning sheet; Text Icon glossary; ba-da-bing instructions	"Build-a-Prompt" sheet; opinion text structures; kernel essay planning sheet; "Planning Thinking" sheet	"Analogy Patterns for Infoshots" sheet	"Three-in-One Infoshots: Try It!" sheet; "Analogy Patterns for Infoshots" sheet	Text structure choices; book report essay planning sheet	Science fair abstract planning sheet; "Informative Text Structures" sheet	"Drive Cam" article; Declaration of Independence example; Hamlet example; text structures from great pieces

Gretchen S. Bernabei · Dottie Hall

The Story of My Thinking

Expository Writing Activities
for 13 Teaching Situations

HEINEMANN
Portsmouth, NH

Heinemann
361 Hanover Street
Portsmouth, NH 03801–3912
www.heinemann.com

Offices and agents throughout the world

The authors and publisher wish to thank those who have generously given permission to reprint borrowed material:

Excerpts from *Common Core State Standards* © Copyright 2010. National Governors Association Center for Best Practices and Council of Chief State School Officers. All rights reserved.

"Watch your driving, kids. The parents are watching." by Matt Zapotosky from *Chicago Tribune*, News Section, 10/26/2008 Issue, Page 8. Copyright © 2008 Chicago Tribune. All rights reserved. Used by permission and protected by the Copyright Laws of the United States. The printing, copying, redistribution, or retransmission of the Material without express written permission is prohibited.

Library of Congress Cataloging-in-Publication Data
Bernabei, Gretchen S.
    The story of my thinking : expository writing activities for 13 teaching situations / Gretchen Bernabei and Dottie Hall.
        p. cm.
    Includes bibliographical references.
    ISBN-13: 978-0-325-04239-8
    ISBN-10: 0-325-04239-X
    1. English language–Composition and exercises–Study and teaching–Activity programs.   2. Exposition (Rhetoric)–Study and teaching–Activity programs.   I. Hall, Dorothy P.   II. Title.
    LB1576.B4835 2012
    372.6–dc23   2012019630

Acquisition editor: Lisa Luedeke
Development editors: Anita Gildea and Tom Newkirk
Production editor: Sonja S. Chapman
Typesetter: Gina Poirier Design
Cover and interior designs: Lisa Fowler
Manufacturing: Steve Bernier

Printed in the United States of America on acid-free paper
16   15   14   13   12   ML   1   2   3   4   5

For Kendall, Matilde, Kelsey, Julian

CONTENTS

Appendix

Works Cited *179*

ACKNOWLEDGMENTS

Tyler Maytum, Danielle Hummel, and Joshua Sellers—three amazing student writers

All the students who have enriched my life

The best mentor and second mom, Pat Gray

The La Fogatians—good food and great company

My principal buddies in Northside ISD

My entire Northside ISD family

My Health Careers High School family

Tom Romano, who planted the indelible moment seed

My parents, who I miss terribly

Terry, Kendall, Kelsey, Blane, and Rosco

Gretchen Bernabei—my best friend and the finest teacher I have ever seen;
you have taught me more than you'll ever know

 —DH

For your editorial guidance and wide-open friendship, Anita Gildea

For your generosity in breakfast conversations, on blogs, in Nings, in hotel lobbies
during conferences, through email, or in the many pieces of writing that you have
shared with us: Carol Jago, Jim Burke, Harry Noden, Harvey Daniels, Barry Lane, Naomi
Shihab Nye, and Thomas Newkirk

For sharing your students with me, and comparing teaching notes:
Stacy Smith, Christine Gonzales, Shannon Blady, Jody Giles, Velma Uriegas, Mindy
Perez, Dave Foss, Kathleen Chupp, Ben Keenan, Ben Chambers, and my roomie,
Charlie Boggess; Macie Bemrick, Lorraine Young, Kipy Alford, Megan Pancone, Gail
Clark, Jayne Hover, Cynthia Candler, Jennifer Koppe, Theresa Phelps, and the
community of the San Antonio Writing Project

For your wonderful drawings, Joe Slagle and Landon Jones

For your inspired leadership and tireless work: P. Tim Martindell, Fort Bend ISD; Rachael Brunson, Round Rock; Janet Charpiot, Mary Endress, Eileen Kress, Katy ISD; Heather Dollins, Granbury; Elizabeth Perez, Edinburg ISD; Greg Reeves, Kay Shurtleff, Cynthia Holcomb, Cindy Tyroff

For your daily goodness: my Eleanor Kolitz family, especially Allison Oakes, Kathryn Davis, Tracy Smith, Michele Sharoni, Melinda Black, Gina Greenfield, Katherine Campbell

For your friendship and brilliance, Lisa Luedeke

For your stunning leadership, Dr. John Folks

For your writing every day, my students past and present

For helping me at home: Alicia Narvaez, Sue King, Judi Reimer, Kim Grauer, Tim King, Sally Aguirre, and Johnny Ponce

And Dottie, all the way back to the very first Spice Girls rubric

—GB

My Inner Turbulence About Expository Writing
and How Carol Jago Helped Me Resolve It

After twenty-five years in the classroom, I can confess that I've had a really bad attitude about expository writing.

I was raised writing five-paragraph essays in the traditional forms, in traditional units of instruction. You've written these too: the descriptive paper; the compare-and-contrast paper; the cause-and-effect paper; the persuasive paper. These are predictable and pure. They start with introductions that unveil the strong thesis statement. They include three body paragraphs. The conclusion reminds the reader of the thesis and repeats it in some new and interesting way. These papers are not messy. They are tidy.

As I grew older, the papers included Kate Turabian–style footnotes and bibliographies, then MLA. These papers grew more sophisticated in syntax, but they left me unthrilled. So did most of the informational, persuasive, and research papers my students wrote. In separating voice and student ownership from the writing, I was asking my students to produce academic-sounding pieces. False pieces.

As a teacher assigning these papers, something else nagged at me: nobody reads papers like these. Not by choice, anyway. Teachers are the only audience of these papers. That may be one of the reasons I thought they were academic.

Then I considered Thomas Newkirk's thought, that real essays "foster and track movement of the mind." This rings true for me, especially when I think about the magazine articles I love to read. They don't follow the structures of the tidy, traditional forms of expository writing units. In fact, tracking movement means there's motion. There's a narrative, even if it's something like a train of thought. This movement satisfies the needs of a reader, offering discovery and maybe some surprises.

So students could use structures that more closely track the movement of their mind, weaving their own slaloms between the twins, knowledge and experience. "I did this, and then this happened, and I thought this, but then this person told me that, so I wondered this, which led me to that, and now I think this." Readers would be more inclined to lean in and vicariously experience that movement of the mind, wouldn't they?

Oh yes, they would. In the foreword to *Strange Bedfellows,* Jim Burke comments: "We read for the conversations that texts invite us to have about the world, human nature, and ourselves. Every text is an invitation to converse and we bring to these encounters a different urgency and perspective at various stages of our lives" (Miller 2008; Foreword by Jim Burke).

But debate arises in the room when teachers compare notes about the validity of student-created text structures and narratives in expository writing. I feel something discordant twanging in me when I hear the lament: "I can't use individualized structures or narrative frames. I don't teach creative writing. I teach academic writing."

Thus crystallized for me a huge piece of my own attitude problem with expository writing. Is high-quality academic writing written only for the eyes of teachers or university professors? Isn't there also rich writing, academic writing, written for voluntary readers, for the general public? What is the role of readers in rigorous, academic writing?

As luck would have it, I found myself having breakfast one morning with Carol Jago, whose voice rang with conviction as she considered my questions:

GB: Do you think there's such a thing as academic writing for an audience, and not just for a teacher?

CJ: The best academic writing is always for an audience. If you don't see the audience, if the audience is just the grade or the score on the test, then it might be a proficient performance, but it's never going to be a great performance. It's never going to be a product you care about. The challenge for us is that right now it's only the kids who grow up in an intellectual family and community who know the pleasure and joys of that kind of writing, thinking, talking. Other students don't have the chance unless their teachers bring it into the classroom. And so we need to bring that kind of scholarly pursuit, that scholarly distinction to our classrooms. The best academic writing is truly argumentative. It's conversational. It's dialogue. Discourse. You can argue something vehemently, effectively, and, at the end of the day, change your mind. That's the kind of thing that makes writing interesting for students, stretching for students, but it's not often done in school. We're caught up in this society, enthralled with test scores and the rest. Teaching kids to do the bare minimum to pass proficiently the state assessment in writing.

GB: So where can you go in the world to find good examples of academic writing? Where's the best place?

CJ: The real world. *The New York Times* op-ed page. David Brooks, Thomas Friedman, Frank Rich, these are great writers. The doctor, Atul Gawande—look at what they do. Michael Pollan. What they do is engaging, conversational, it's full of anecdote and storytelling—talk about narrative writing. All of this is academic writing.

GB: You would consider those academic, even though they're not written in MLA format?

CJ: Oh yeah. Those are the essays that make a difference in the world. Often things that appear in MLA format are just for other academics. Talk about no audience. Is that a real audience? Just when you're talking to people just like you?

GB: Why do I keep thinking that academic writing for other academicians is the only real form of academic writing?

CJ: I think we created that dichotomy ourselves by not thinking hard enough about the larger world. A true scholar should be intent also upon changing the world, not just about getting tenure. Not just about getting a good grade. True scholars are so passionate about what they know that they know that they need to take it out to the world. I think Michael Pollan is one of the best examples. There's one botanist who has changed the world.

After Carol went on her way, I thought about what she had said. I realized that I'd been operating from some sort of archaic, English-teachery view of academic writing, and that I needed, as Carol said, to think harder about the larger world. I thought also about how the world has changed.

I thought about TED talks. About Sir Ken Robinson's TED talk about creativity, in particular. If you haven't heard it, google it! Of course his discourse was academic. And it was also delightful and thought-provoking, not at all dry, dense, or hard to choke down.

But still, I felt secretly hypocritical when I faced a classroom of young and developing students, all of whom I wanted to prepare for college-level writing. How would I move them toward this level? For developing writers, must creativity and analysis be mutually exclusive?

My Self-Inflicted Confusion About Personality in Academic Writing, and How Thomas Newkirk Helped Me Reframe It

One day I asked Thomas Newkirk a similar question, trying to put my finger on whatever sore spot was creating my conflict. Shouldn't the student's personality be absent in academic writing? He chuckled and answered, "Only in bad academic writing." I realized in an instant my confusion, contained in the chuckle of a distinguished academician: rigor doesn't mean students must write badly.

Personality isn't the same as level of formality, Dr. Newkirk explained. "Personality is one of your tools, and if you say I'm going to be impersonal, you've lost one of your great tools as a writer. It's a lie that academic writing means you have to dispense with your personality. My enthusiasm, my passion for things, there's a place for that in analytic writing. There's a necessity for it. That's what sustains us as readers and writers."

So how do we teach that?

My Secret Balking over Pure (Fake) Forms of Expository Writing and How Harvey Daniels Helped Me See Through It

Students walk into every classroom boisterous or subdued, but filled with their own enthusiasms and passions. How do we harness all that student-ness for writing really good expository pieces? How do we break down this process and convert it to concrete steps for students?

I ponder the structures we'll need to use for expository writing. Personal narratives are a snap to organize, since they're basically sequential. But what about expository writing? Writing information, or literary analysis, or persuasive arguments?

Jerome Bruner divides the two ways that we talk about what we know: logico-scientific thinking, about physical things, and narrative thinking, about people and situations. Should I separate these for classroom focus? Usually we have a more delightful experience in classes when our students are writing their experiences in their personal narratives, and if I knew how to mesh the two processes more effectively, my attitude toward analytic writing might improve.

Harvey Daniels' voice has been ringing in my ear since a 2002 *Voices from the Middle* article when he pointed out that these "pure" forms of expository writing are not what we find in newspapers:

> As we read further into these three articles, we find much more complex, diverse, and recursive organizational patterns than the trusty old curriculum guides led us to expect. There is a welter of structures used in each piece, with the authors seeming to slide between one and another, a paragraph at a time, without warning. After an opening vignette, there might be a paragraph listing some items of import, followed by another vignette, told chronologically; then there might be the posing of a problem and some possible solutions, followed by a sequence of past events, a list of examples just piled on top of each other, and then still more narrative. All these articles seem to be organizational hybrids; nothing is simple or straightforward. (9)

Organizational hybrids. His focus was on reading, but his observations have powerful implications for writing, as well. Writing organizational hybrids is a pretty serious goal. How do we aim students toward those?

And before organizing their thoughts, students face an even more daunting task. How do they get thoughts to organize? How do we get students to generate content? To come up with stuff? Often we teachers sidestep this question and hand students predigested topics. I can hear student questions: "What do you want me to write about?" "What do you want it to sound like?" "What do you want me to say about this topic?" "How long does it need to be?" Sometimes I have to suppress an urge to make up crazy answers. But if we really want the students to do the composing, we cannot hand them answers to all of those questions, or we are the composers. They ask these questions because they want to do it right.

My Own Inner Turmoil About Canned Expository Units and How James Moffett Helped Me Replace Them

So our task evolves. We need to find a way to help students unearth their own topics, to generate plenty of content, and to organize it so that readers can track the movement of the writer's mind.

And then I turn to The Book on my teaching bookshelf. There it is, blue and tattered. William Strong called it "the Rosetta stone" for English teachers, James

Moffett's *Teaching the Universe of Discourse*. And once again, in it I find exactly what I need:

> In interior dialogue we have subjective, spontaneous, inchoate beginnings of drama (what is happening), narrative (what happened), exposition (what happens), and argumentation (what may happen). As it bears on curriculum, this means that students would tap, successively, their inner streams of sensations, memories, and ideas, as raw material for recordings, narrative reports, and essays of generalization and theory. (1968, 40)

As I digest this passage, I write notes:

Drama—what is happening

Narrative—what happened

Exposition—what happens

Argumentation—what may happen

If we could tap a student's inner thought stream, theoretically, one memory, one sensory reaction, or one idea could provide raw material for any kind of writing, just by jiggling the verb tense. I think about quick lists, kernel essays, and indelible moments that we've already been using, and the floodgates open.

As I feel that clamoring hope, the Young Frankenstein Gene Wilder voice rises in me, "This . . . could . . . work!" And I wish, for the thousandth time, that I could thank James Moffett.

My Lingering Qualms About Assessing Opinion Writing and Calling It Informative, and How the Common Core State Standards Helped Me Make Peace with It

Many of our state assessments ask younger students to write about their opinions (e.g., their favorite person, day, pet). Different states label this kind of writing in different ways, and it has bothered me. Isn't it important for our students to be able to distinguish between information and opinion?

Then I absorbed this from the Common Core State Standards on developing writers:

> Although young children are not able to produce fully developed logical arguments, they develop a variety of methods to extend and elaborate their work by providing examples, offering reasons for their assertions, and

explaining cause and effect. These kinds of expository structures are steps on the road to argument. In grades K–5, the term "opinion" is used to refer to this developing form of argument. (Appendix A, 23)

So if we're asking students to tell us an opinion, we are asking for an assertion, or argument, in its fledgling state. By asking them to explain plenty about why they have that opinion, they are doing quite a bit of informing. The important thing is that they have plenty of chances to write about topics that are meaningful to them, in a variety of ways, for a variety of situations. Then they will be ready for tests.

An Overview of What We Know About the Writing Process

These steps may not happen sequentially, but they include:

1. **Generating content that satisfies an itch**

   In any really good piece of writing, there is some satisfaction that happens between the reader and the writer, some need being addressed. Various kinds of writing have various kinds of dynamics. The more sharply the itch is felt, the more urgent is the writing.

2. **Finding a structure that serves the writer and reader**

   Students move from structures that are teacher-chosen to student-chosen, to student-created. Well-wrought structures move a reader through the writer's thoughts, creating a chance for the reader to "track the movement of the mind" of the writer. The writer designs that experience for the reader and composes a kernel essay, a short version of the reader's journey.

3. **Detailing the writing through a combination of strategies**

   Students flesh out the short version with snapshots, thoughtshots, sensory details, dialogue, and various other types of information.

4. **Selecting the genre for delivery to the audience**

   Students tailor the writing to suit the requirements of the form for their writing. In a *Framework for Success in Postsecondary Writing,* a coalition of writing educators urges us to prepare students for college by designing writing:

   > with genuine purposes and audiences in mind (from teachers and other students to community groups, local or national officials, commercial interests, students' friends and relatives, and other potential readers) in order to foster flexibility and rhetorical versatility. Standardized writing curricula or assessment instruments that emphasize formulaic writing for nonauthentic audiences will not reinforce the habits of mind and the experiences necessary for success as students encounter the writing demands of postsecondary education. (2011, 3)

So how do we enter into this process in our classrooms? What do we do first? What if it's October and we have done other things first? Oh no, I'm midstream, my population is diverse: four needy, three dysgraphic, seven ADHD, two behaviorally scary, four low-level, three newcomers, four so gifted I'm bonkers. And three absent.

How to Use This Book

In *Holding On to Good Ideas in a Time of Bad Ones,* Thomas Newkirk (2009) says that "teaching is profoundly situational." Knowing that, we have based the chapters on teaching situations you could find yourself in. The one truth that does not change for us teachers, ever, is that there is never enough time.

So this book is for teachers who need a lesson but don't have time to read a book before applying it. We've based the lessons on teaching situations, because it really does depend. Feel free to dip in and out of lessons; flip to the glossary if you need a refresher about what a kernel essay is; use the chart instead of the pages if you like; adapt at your leisure.

For each lesson, you'll find a description of the teaching situation followed by the summary of the lesson. In the next section, "Teaching It," we've included a transcript of what you'd see if you walked into our classrooms and saw us teaching this lesson. Does that mean you must teach it identically? Only if you're doing comedy. Of course it's not a script for you to follow, but a model that we offer. It's a glimpse into our classrooms. Your classroom is uniquely yours, and we hope you share glimpses back with us.

Students work best when they have choices. Clearly, the same is true of teachers. So with all of this attitude change swimming in my head, my colleague Dottie Hall and I have committed to helping every teacher think about how you approach analytic writing with your students. We hope you will be as energized by the process as we have been.

1

Indelible Moments

If You Want to Begin with Heartfelt Moments from the Students' Lives

Basic Steps

1. Write indelible moment #1
2. Write indelible moment #2
3. Write indelible moment #3
4. Choose one to expand
5. Make a before and after tri-fold
6. Design a frame for it

Tool

- "Objects to Use" list

Setting the Scene

The moment you begin to talk about a writing assignment, your students get a glazed look, sluggish, dazed, tired. You'd like to pull from them something dazzling, something wonderful, something effortless. This activity almost seems like play, and the results are actually surprisingly dazzling.

The Point

Tom Romano (2000) writes that "Bright moments are indelible. They are happiness, joy and ecstasy. Life without them would be bleak." These indelible moments can also be sad or painful. But one way to tap those indelible moments is with different kinds of paper. By giving students a unique kind of paper (telephone message pad page, a paper plate, coffee filter, moving tag) and a question about their indelible moments, students can write on these objects with enthusiasm. And indelible moments emerge in writing, ready for use in all kinds of ways.

Teaching It

Figure 1–1
Blank telephone message pad page

"Do you know what indelible ink is? That's right, it's ink that can't be erased. It's permanent. One of my favorite writers says that we have indelible moments in our lives, too, moments that we always remember, whether it's because they're happy or sad."

"What I am going to ask you to do right now is to take a minute and think about indelible phone conversations that you have had. You can write one either on the blank message pad page if you want to or on a separate piece of paper. But think for just a minute. Write an indelible phone conversation."

(Give them a few minutes to write, and then share. After sharing, put these aside.)

Debriefing

- "Did you have any trouble thinking of an indelible moment?"
- "Did writing it on the message pad change what you remembered about that indelible moment?"

What to Do Next

- On a subsequent day, do a different indelible moment. Write, share, and put these aside.
- On another subsequent day, do one more indelible moment. Write, share, and put these aside.

Now that there are three, students will choose one to expand into a longer essay. They may expand it by using a text structure or by completing a tri-fold:

▶ DIRECTIONS FOR A TRI-FOLD

Simply fold a piece of paper in three equal parts. On the left side write the words, "Before the moment." In the middle section, write the words, "The indelible moment," and in the third section, write the words, "After the moment."

Students need to write the indelible moment in the center section; on the left part, they need to think and write about what happened before that indelible moment. Next, on the right part, they need to write about what happened after the moment. After completing the tri-fold, kids will share the writing in groups of four or five.

Spin-offs

- Have students rewrite the moments into different genres (see following examples) for variety.
- Have students write flashback frames for their indelible moments (see Tyler's example, following).
- Use these for literature analysis by having students choose a character's indelible moment, write it, and say how they chose that moment as indelible to the character.
- Convert these (personal narrative) moments to expository pieces via the elastic kernel activity in Chapter 3.

Student Samples

Phil, a sixth grader, remembered an indelible phone conversation that brought a new pet to his family (Figure 1–2, below right).

This student remembered a self-induced prank call (Figure 1–3, below left).

Figure 1–2 Grade 6 phone message, "Dog"

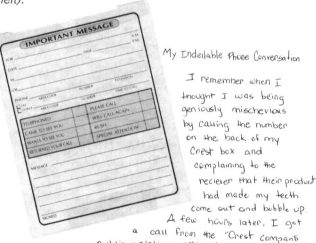

My Indelible Phone Conversation

I remember when I thought I was being geniously mischevious by calling the number on the back of my Crest box and complaining to the reciever that their product had made my teeth come out and bubble up. A few hours later, I got a call from the "Crest companys public relations officer" who informed me that they were going to have to sue me for harassment of the company employees. Several minutes into the conversation, after he had asked many questions about my personal information and me in complete hysterics and panic, the voice at the other end of the phone begin to laugh, so loud, in fact, that I could hear it coming from down stairs! Upon desending to the first floor, I turned to find my father turning red with laughter. I learned that day to stick to Colgate.

Figure 1–3 Grade 12 phone message, "Crest"

Figure 1–4
Paper plate with indelible moment, "First Date"

Danielle Hummel, grade 12, recalled a moment involving a meal.

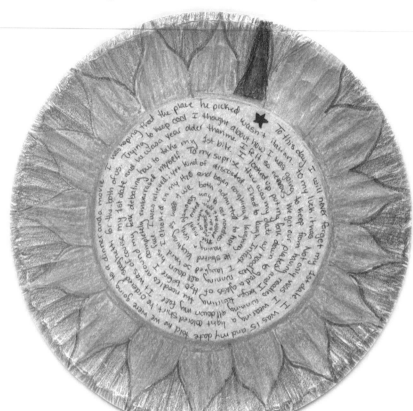

Objects to Use for Indelible Moment Writing

1. Using the pink phone pad paper, write about an indelible phone conversation.
2. Using the lined paper, write about an indelible moment from school.
3. Using the coffee filter, write about an indelible conversation you shared while having a cup of coffee.
4. Using the moving tag, write about an indelible moment involving packing or unpacking.
5. Using the birthday card, write about an indelible birthday memory.
6. Using the paper plate, write about an indelible moment that took place during dinner.
7. Using this invitation, write about an indelible moment at a party.
8. Using this wrapping paper, write about an indelible moment involving a gift.
9. Using this note card, write about an indelible moment involving a letter.
10. Using this thank-you note, write about an indelible moment when you said thank you to someone or someone said thank you to you.
11. Using this graduation paper, write about an indelible moment in high school.
12. On the sports page of this newspaper, write about an indelible moment that involves sports.

Teachers used primary-style composition paper to recall indelible moments from their school days.

It was my first day in the US. Eighth grade last six weeks. A kid took me from the counselors office to my first period class. It was Math. I got paired with a Mexican girl who barely knew Spanish. The teacher showed an algebraic equation on an overhead projector titled warm-up. She was seeking the answer. I sat down raised my hand and showed her with body language and a small "me . . . me" coming out of my frightened lips. She was surprised, she aloud me to come to the overhead and work the problem, my steps to solving the equation were different than what she had been teaching her class. I came up with the right answer. The teacher knew not to question my process, she know only to revise my answers. From that point on I was the Colombian girl who did not know English but knew how to do Algebra.

—Yolanda Cáceres de Ramos

The 1970 Jordanian Civil War started, for me, one bright sunny day in May during PE class. As usual, my forth grade class of 12 and the equally small class of fifth graders were playing a riveting game of soccer when we heard "Blam! Whoosh! Blam! Blam!" Unexperienced, we didn't immediately respond, but continued kicking and passing the ball. Then our teacher yelled, "Drop down! On the ground!" he had a sense of urgency and complete sincerity, even fear, in his commanding voice. Following his lead we crawled the 50 yards, to the safe school building, responding bullets whizzing overhead.

School finished early that year!

—Jo N. Hemingway

I was never one to take naps. In kindergarten, that was something they expected us to do, so naturally I had a hard time doing it. That's probably why Mrs. Ames put me in the back—me and Tina. Tina and I had many delightfully stimulating conversations during nap-time, whispering in the back like she couldn't hear us! One day Mrs. Ames left the room for a minute—probably to run to the restroom, and I decided that that meant I should help her out and check to make sure that everyone was napping appropriately. In my denim Osh Kosh 'B Gosh overalls with strawberries on them, I quietly got up and proceeded to walk around the room checking on everyone. I'd gotten all the way to Darwin Thomas in the middle of the room when Mrs. Ames walked back in. If you're going to be sneaky at nap-time, make sure you have a look-out!

—Stephanie Dickens

These are samples of indelible moments retold in other genres.

Limerick
—Antoinette Boulet

Mrs. Wyman taught us Sex Ed
She looked like she'd rather be dead
She admitted sex was great
Only to procreate
But no one believed what she said!

Moving Memory to Advertisement
—Mary Dawson

Earplugs for the loud, trashy neighbors below you	$5.50
Paint for the marks left by the maintenance man trying to get rid of the snake on the balcony	$25.00
Bail money to pay the court for keying your selfish neighbor's car	$100.00
The deed to your first home	Priceless

Menu—Going to College
—Janae Miles

APPETIZER

Gift Cards	$25, $50, $100
Boxes	$0
Tape	$5
Hangers	$10
Luggage	$50

MAIN COURSE

Family	Price Negotiable
Roommate	$25–$100
Dorm Room	$2,500
Guys w/ strong arms	$50

SIDE DISHES

Kleenex	$5
Double-sided tape	$5
Cell phone	$100

DESSERT

Saying good-bye	Priceless

Dictionary Entry

Lifesaver: A person who somehow knows just what you need and when you need it; example—a phone call from a loving, reassuring voice when you are having a really rough day.

—*Kim Warwick*

Thank-You Note

—*Lee James*

Dear restaurant patron,

Thank you for visiting our fine establishment last night. When I introduced myself and asked how you were this evening, thank you for responding, "Diet Coke." Thank you for inventing foods not on our menu and then complaining about your own inventions. Thank you for sending your glass of wine back because it wasn't the right bottle. When the bartender poured you a new glass from the exact same bottle, you smugly thanked me for getting it right. No, thank you.

Sample of an indelible moment, detailed into an essay.

The Rawlings leather was on fire as the ball came off my bat in a rush. It was almost like a fighter jet racing off the launch pad. Somewhere in the middle of the ball's flight I began to think about what got me here.

I met Nick when I was fifteen years old during my freshman year in high school. He came to O'Connor to be our summer baseball league coach. "You guys out here at O'Connor have talent, you just need a coach to help you progress," he said "and I'm here to help you guys do that."

The look in Steve's eyes was a sickening look. As I approached him I saw a tear come from his eyes when he said, "Tyler, Nick passed away early this morning." Everything seemed to go silent. You could hear a pin drop in the cafeteria. Steve said something else, but I just watched his lips move, nothing was going through my head except for Nick. Nick and his four-year-old son, his newborn son, his poor wife.

And just as these thoughts came to a screeching halt, the ball hit outside the left field fence. I had waited on the curve just like I was taught to do. As I began to trot to first base, I realized this was the beginning of my journey in the game of baseball without Nick. I was from that point on, on my own.

—*Tyler Maytum, grade 12*

TEACHER TALK: This is the actual indelible moment that Tyler started with. He then added the detail for the rest of the story during drafting. He also added the frame, the bat hitting the ball in the beginning, and the ball sailing in the ending frame.

2 Personal Narrative with Reflection

If You Want Them to Write
Tightly Focused Memories
with a Reflective Layer

Basic Steps

1. Create a quick list
2. Kernel essay #1 (write/share)
3. Kernel essay #2 (write/share)
4. Kernel essay #3 (write/share)
5. Choose one
6. Add details
7. Interrogate the moment

Tool

- Kernel essay planning sheet

Setting the Scene

You would like to start off with personal narratives. You might be thinking about easing your students into their writing, since people have an easier time writing about their own experiences than about the rest of the world. But you'd really like for them to dig a little deeper in search of something more interesting than "a special time" or "a favorite time" or "an unforgettable memory." And you'd really like to find a way to narrow their focus to one brief time, not an era in their lives.

What follows is a sequence of three lessons that accomplish these goals.

Step One: **Make a Quick List of Important Moments in Your Life**

The Point

Students have a difficult time beginning to write an essay. Since memories can provide the most accessible content, they are a great starting place. This activity builds for students a bank of moments to use for many kinds of writing, not just personal narratives.

Teaching It

"Remember the two hands, the ones that show what you know and how you know it? Today we're going to start with the left hand and create a list of memories you might use. We'll share later, so while we're working on our lists, please don't share yet."

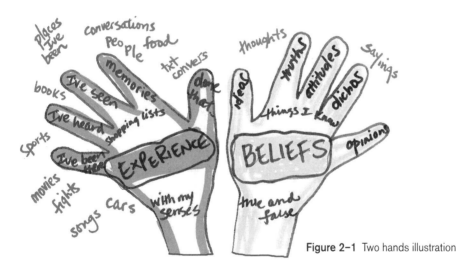

Figure 2–1 Two hands illustration

- "Title your paper 'Quick List of Moments.'"
- "Number your paper from one to ten."
- "Think about the differences between short moments and long periods of time. For this list, use only the short moments."

(Wait until everyone is ready.)

- "For numbers one, two, and three, write down moments when you were completely proud of someone else, not yourself." *(Model on an overhead or whiteboard.)*

Quick List of Moments
(the time that...)

proud
of
some-
one
else
1. Matilde's Batboy last song
2. Mom: a duck that isn't funny
3. the Second Wind tour

Struggle
4. losing Jiminy Cricket
5. missing lunch w/ Chris Goode
6. Bob's phone call

animal
7. whomping Marigold
8. Daisy, Julian & Jennifer

Clothing
9. the pumpkin Skirt
10.

- "For numbers four, five, and six, write down moments in your life that were a struggle for you, any kind of struggle. You lived through those moments, but they were tough." *(Model on an overhead.)*

- "For numbers seven and eight, write down moments involving an animal (or reptile, bird, insect, mammal, pet, whatever you'd like to use)." *(Model on an overhead.)*

- "For nine and ten, write down unfortunate (or surprising, happy, etc.) clothing moments (or hair, shoe, teeth, etc.)." *(Model on an overhead.)*

Figure 2–2
Quick List of
Moments example

Debriefing

- "Was that difficult or easy?"
- "Did your moments pop up more easily on some of the categories than on others? Which?"

Step Two: **Write a Kernel Essay**

The Point

Sometimes when students sit down to write up a memory, they don't know how far back to begin, how much family philosophy to include first, how much character description to add before launching into the actual moment. And so the results can have a multitude of serious problems. Some writing wanders; some is too vague; some is too short. This guided writing exercise familiarizes students with the format of a kernel essay, while precluding this whole range of problems.

Fig. 2–3
"A Memory" text
structure

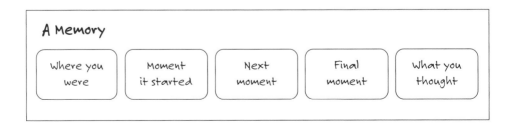

A Memory

| Where you were | Moment it started | Next moment | Final moment | What you thought |

Teaching It

"Today you're going to write a kernel essay."

- "First, choose a moment from your quick list, a moment you wouldn't mind everyone hearing all about."
- "Number your paper one through five. Skip lines between the numbers."
- "I'm going to ask you five questions about that moment. All you have to do is just answer the questions as simply as you can, using complete sentences."
- "Before we begin, think about the memory that you chose. Let it replay in your mind for a moment. It's almost like a little movie, isn't it? It's a little story."
- "Number one: Where were you?" *(Give the students a few minutes to write. On the overhead, show the first box of "A Memory" text structure.)*
- "Number two: What happened first?" *(Give the students a few minutes to write. On the overhead, show the second box of "A Memory" text structure.)*
- "Number three: What happened next?" *(Give the students a few minutes to write. On the overhead, show the third box of "A Memory" text structure.)*
- "Number four: What happened last?" *(Give the students a few minutes to write. On the overhead, show the fourth box of "A Memory" text structure.)*
- "Number five: What's one life lesson that this moment brought you? Begin it with 'I've learned that . . .'" *(Give the students a few minutes to write. On the overhead, show the fifth box of "A Memory" text structure.)*

"You have now written a kernel essay. Let's hear some." *(Share either with groups or partners, or with volunteers in the large group, and debrief.)*

What to Do Next

- Share and put aside.
- On a subsequent day, choose another moment from the quick list, and guide the students through another kernel essay, the same way. Share and put aside.
- On a subsequent day, choose another moment from the quick list, and guide the students through another kernel essay, the same way. Share and put aside.
- Now that students have written several kernel essays, have them copy the structure into what will become their own personal collection of useful structures. I have them do this in the back of their journals.
- Next, choose one of the kernels to flesh out into a full essay.
- Add details (see the icon glossary in the back).

Debriefing

- "Are you surprised at what you wrote?"
- "Are you astounded by the power of what you heard?"
- "Can you believe that all this was accomplished in five simple sentences?"
- "Can you explain how these short pieces can contain so much power?"
- "How would you expand these sentences to become a full essay? What would you add?"

Spin-offs

Have students rewrite their kernel essay as a different genre.

Fig. 2–4
Kernel essay planning sheet

Name: _____

Planning Sheet

Type of Writing (Check One)
☐ Writing about myself   ☐ Writing to inform me   ☐ Writing to inform others   ☐ Writing to persuade   ☐ Writing about literature

Put your **truism** (aka assertion aka problem aka main question) here.
_____
_____

Put your **text structure** here.

☐ ☐ ☐ ☐ ☐ ☐

Write your **kernel essay** here.
1. _____
2. _____
3. _____
4. _____
5. _____
6. _____

Plan for **details**:

ACTION DETAIL		INFOSHOTS	
☐ snapshots	☐ sensory details	☐ description	☐ synonyms/antonyms
☐ thoughtshots	☐ ba-da-bing	☐ compare/contrast	☐ part/whole
☐ dialogue	☐ _____	☐ cause/effect	☐ item/category
		☐ before/after	☐ _____

TEACHER TALK: Students may register frustration that they need more "what happened next" sentences before the "what happened last" sentence. Allow them to write more, expanding this structure. You can name this new structure after the first student who needed more sentences, and post it along with your original on the wall of structures.

Step Three: Interrogate the Experience for Deeper Reflection

The Point

Often student narratives may supply details about moments in their lives but no deep introspection about the meaning of that moment. While the writing may be lovely, it's not really analytic. Therefore, it's more like a well-written diary entry than an essay. This exercise asks students to write one more chunk in which they freely interrogate the experience.

Teaching It

(Give students a large index card, sticky note, or a half-sheet of paper and their personal narratives.) "You have written up a moment. Now it's time to step back and think about that moment. I'd like to ask you to write one more bit. Ask yourself, what questions does this experience raise for me? What questions does it answer? How has this moment helped me become who I was then, or who I am now? Your writing does not have to be a cohesive paragraph at all, just your thoughts as you ponder what that moment meant to your changing self."

(Place these questions where the students can see them as they think and write.)

Questions for Thoughtful Reflection About a Memory

Ask yourself:
- Why did you pick this moment?
- What part of your personality has changed because of this moment?
- Which of your values became clearer because of this moment?
- How was this moment a pivot point in your life?
- Now, looking back, what do you see that you didn't see before?
- What questions did this moment raise for me?
- What questions did this moment answer?
- How has this moment helped me become who I was then? Or who I am now?

"Share."

Debriefing

- "Could you add this part to your essay? Where would it go? (The beginning, the end, part in each?)"
- "How would this part change the essay to a reader's eyes?"

Student Samples

Sample kernel essays:

1. At the beach, I was feeding seagulls chex-mix.
2. I was mad at the seagulls so I threw sand at it.
3. The seagull got angry so it swooped down and I fell on the ground.
4. It kind of bit on my ear and it hurt.
5. You shouldn't mess with a seagull, cause he's gonna get you.

—Mac Meissner, grade 6

1. I was at our old house in New York, and I was watching the construction men.
2. My mom was trying to get our old dog, Scout, up into our house, which was being raised seven feet due to flooding.
3. Since there was no staircase and dogs couldn't climb ladders, we had to construct a pulley.
4. We all had to hoist Scout up on to our house. We were all laughing hard, but Scout loved it.
5. No matter what life throws at you, you have to think of a way to counter it.

—Jack E., grade 6

1. Again alone, I'm driving down the streets of Corpus Christi.
2. I spot a group of druggies, hoping that one might be my daughter.
3. Frightened, I slowly drove up and showed them a picture of Nilda, asked if they'd seen her, but to no avail.
4. I'm crushed, heart broken, unable to breath, but I head home anyway.
5. As difficult as it may be, a mom has to give up, let go, and let God.

—Belinda Childs, teacher

1. I was sitting in my car, gripping the steering wheel, trying not to cry, as I waved goodbye. I told my parents, "I'll be fine."

2. I hooked a left onto Shoreham Drive and tears uncontrollably ran down my face.

3. I drove for 25 hours straight only stopping to get gas and eat.

4. At 5:00 a.m., I pulled into the driveway of my new life.

5. Even though you don't always know what 5:01 a.m. will bring, the sun will still rise and you have to go on with your life!

—*Christina Stroff, teacher*

Robert develops his kernel with details (see text icons on pages 143–144 for detailing ideas).

Death Causes Pain

My heart was beating as we opened up the garage door leading into my garage. Salty sweat still dripped from my face as we pulled in. we had just had our first victory of our 8th grade football season. We were down by a touchdown late in the fourth quarter when we got the ball back and the momentum changed in our favor. I was the tail back and ran the ball up the middle for a few yard gain. We did that for the next few plays. The clock was now running down just under two minutes when we faked the play to me up the middle, like we had been doing in the passed plays, and handed the ball of the Justin Latimer running around the outside corner and scored. The crowd went wild as we went up by 2 after getting the 2-point conversion. It was probably one of the better games we have played and excitement reeked from my body and we came to a stop in the garage. Little did I know all of that excitement was about to be turned into sadness.

The car had just come to a stop and the roaring engine shut off after my mom turned the keys to the left and pulled them out of the ignition. I opened the door and hoped out onto the garage ground when my mom stopped my in my tracks. "Honey, Cheyanne died this morning . . . " I didn't know what to say back to that, so I just stared into her eyes. Silence fell over my body as I stood there. It felt like my body weight had increased 20 pounds. I didn't know what to think and I blankly stared straight at my garage door leading to my back-yard where my dog loved to sleep and thought to myself that she would never ever be there again.

"Wait, what? Why didn't you tell me?" I said as tears began to flood my eyes and run down my face. I felt disappointed as to why she didn't tell me when it actually did happen and why she is just now telling me this. My throat started to swell up as the salty taste came into my mouth of tears from my eyes. "Why was she dying?" I thought to myself, "she was in such good shape." Then something hit me. What was Chris, my brother, going to say about this. Cheyanne was his dog and he had been through so much with her. How was Chris going to react to this happening? How was mom even taking this? I'm sure this was hard of her, she had to get rid of the body.

"I didn't want you to be sad all day and for your game" she said as her face started to look more dull. Are you kidding me? I don't care if I was going to be sad all day, I would like to know when my dog died at the moment it happened. I had no idea what to say back to that so I simply just closed the door and walked to the house door and opened it and walked inside. My eyes we starting to become really fuzzy and blurry now. I walked into my room, lay on my bed, buried my head in the pillows, and cried.

I learned that something happen in life and just sitting there and acting depressed about it wont get you past it at all. You have to look past it. Sometimes you have to get over things and move on to the next day.

—*Robert Schuler, grade 9*

In this memory, Laura ends with a powerful extended metaphor.

The tires and engine whirred harmoniously as my mother's car glided smoothly across the black asphalt road of my surrounding neighborhood. "This is freedom," I thought, reaching over to change the radio station to whatever I wanted: at that moment, the options felt endless.

It was a clear, cloudless Monday afternoon, seemingly like any other, but this specific Monday was the Monday I'd gotten my driver's license. I had finally been granted the freedom to turn down any road I wished, listen to *my* radio stations, and be in control of my arrival time to various social events, and for me, it felt like getting to choose my destiny.

However, this power of freedom and destiny in the hands of a rosy-cheeked sixteen-year-old does not always lead to a happy ending.

As I executed a smooth curve along the narrow expanse of Contour Drive, my car, this symbol of liberty, shuddered, sputtered, and made very possible noise a car should *not* make. I quickly veered to the side of the road, managing to get out of the flow of traffic safely. I then rapidly dialed my mom, listened to a lecture about the advantages of actually having gas in the gas tank, and proceeded to wait, humiliated, as the towers towed my downtrodden-looking liberty to the nearest gas station.

My experience resounds through my memories, reminding me not only that cars require gas, but that with the blessing of freedom, comes the weight of responsibility. Like a baby bird, I was not ready to jump out of the comforting nest and fly, but I should enjoy the spreading of my wings, until the wind is right for me to fly.

—*Laura Krueger, grade 11*

3 Elastic Essays from Narratives

If You Want to Start with the Personal Narrative They Just Wrote

Basic Steps

1. Write titles using elastic topic
2. Choose aim
3. Choose structure
4. Write kernel
5. Add details

Tools

- Elastic kernel activity sheet
- "Titles That Sell" sheet

Setting the Scene

Your students have written personal narratives, and now you are turning your attention to expository writing. The writing was truly about the students, so you found the reading interesting and lively. You hate to lose those qualities, but as you peruse your teaching materials, the expository materials leave you a little cold. The topics suggested seem sterile. You'd like to keep your classroom momentum and energy moving into expository writing. And you can.

The Point

After students have written essays (or even kernel essays) about memories, this exercise helps them explore possibilities for turning those memory pieces into informative or persuasive writing.

Teaching It

- "Students, we have listened to your memory kernel essays. Now we're going to stretch these to see what all they can become."

- "Let's start with Parker's memory about catching a marlin." *(Read this or another kernel essay.)*

> We were deep-sea fishing.
> We hooked a marlin.
> We brought in the marlin.
> We tagged and released the marlin.
> Some moments stay with you forever.

- "Now, it's true that this is his memory. Let's see . . . how can this topic become informational? What all might someone want to know about? Let's list everything we think up. (*Model thinking up a list, adding any ideas students volunteer.*) Hmm . . . All about marlins . . . how to catch one . . . how to book a fishing trip like that . . . where you go . . . all about how fishing for large fish like this is different from fishing in a fishing hole . . . how that catch-and-release thing works with an electronic tag . . . maybe safety tips for deep-sea fishing. Any of those would be interesting pieces, filled with information."

- "How could any of this become persuasive? Persuasive . . . what people think and why they should think differently . . . to get people to *do* something. Let's list everything we can think of." (*Model thinking up a list, adding any ideas students volunteer.*) "Okay, how about . . . why people should participate in the tag-and-release activities . . . or why families should spend more time out on the water together, or how the gulf waters should be protected from more oil spills, or why all young men should go deep-sea fishing with their fathers?"

- "See how this works?"

- "Now let's see what you come up with. On the elastic kernel page, write down what your memory is about, what subject. Then see if you can fill in some ideas in the other columns."

(Distribute the elastic kernel sheet; let them work on it, and share out as they make progress.)

Figure 3–1 Elastic kernel activity sheet

Titles That Sell Informational Articles

All About _____ and Why It Matters

Everything You Need to Know About _____

What You Never Knew About _____

Top Ten Reasons for _____

The Secret(s) Behind _____

The Truth About _____

Amazing Facts About _____

The Real Story About _____

The _____ Controversy

Your Personal Guide to _____

Success with _____

Win Big with _____

Prizewinning _____

The Ultimate Scoop on _____

Hidden Secrets About _____

An Essential Guide to _____

The Zen of _____

_____ for Dummies

Lessons from a _____

Just Say No to _____

Little Known Facts About _____

The Secret Life of _____

Figure 3–2 Titles That Sell

Name: _____

Planning Sheet

Type of Writing (Check One)
☐ Writing about myself ☐ Writing to inform me ☐ Writing to inform others ☐ Writing to persuade ☐ Writing about literature

Put your **truism** (aka assertion aka problem aka main question) here
_____

Put your **text structure** here
[ ] [ ] [ ] [ ] [ ]

Write your **kernel essay** here
1. _____
2. _____
3. _____
4. _____
5. _____
6. _____

Plan for **details**

ACTION DETAIL
☐ snapshots ☐ sensory details
☐ thoughtshots ☐ ba-da-bing
☐ dialogue ☐ _____

INFOSHOTS
☐ description ☐ synonyms/antonyms
☐ compare/contrast ☐ part/whole
☐ cause/effect ☐ item/category
☐ before/after ☐ _____

Figure 3–3 Kernel essay planning sheet

- "If you picture the articles from magazines, you can picture some titles for these columns. Take a look at this page of titles and see if you can write at least four titles for informative and persuasive writing. You don't need to write any articles or essays yet, just titles."

(Distribute the "Titles That Sell" page, and give them a little more time. Share a couple of early finishers to help the others who need models from their peers.)

- "Now it's time to get into groups and listen to each other's titles."

Debriefing

- "How are informative and persuasive writing different?"
- "Is it fair to mix personal narratives with informative or persuasive writing?"

What to Do Next

Have students choose one of the titles to write.

On a planning sheet:

Write the title.

Select a structure.

Write a kernel essay.

Flesh it out with details.

Name: _____

Elastic Kernel

Your Topic: _____

How could you write about this topic in different ways?

NARRATIVE (What Happened)	EXPOSITORY (What Hapened)	ARGUMENTATION (What Should Happen)
Memory driven: what happened in your life, and what did it mean to you?	**Curiosity driven:** what would other people want to know? What else would you want to find out?	**Driven by the need for change:** right/wrong, good/better, current ways/better ways
Ex: The moment that we caught a marlin	**All about** fishing tackle How to catch a marlin **Different kinds** of fishing trips **Background on** catch-and-release **Tips for** safe fishing	**Why** catch-and-release is important **Why** families **should** fish together **Why** gulf waters **should** be protected The value of male bonding over fishing **The benefits of** spending time with your family out in nature

Figure 3–4 Elastic Kernel Essay planning sheet

Titles That Sell Informational Articles

All About _____ and Why It Matters

Everything You Need to Know About _____

What You Never Knew About _____

Top Ten Reasons for _____

The Secret(s) Behind _____

The Truth About _____

Amazing Facts About _____

The Real Story About _____

The _____ Controversy

Your Personal Guide to _____

Success with _____

Win Big with _____

Prizewinning _____

The Ultimate Scoop on _____

Hidden Secrets About _____

An Essential Guide to _____

The Zen of _____

_____ for Dummies

Lessons from a _____

Just Say No to _____

Little Known Facts About _____

The Secret Life of _____

Figure 3–5 "Titles That Sell" informational articles

Student Samples

Name Barrett

Elastic Kernel

Your topic: The time I broke my arm

How could you write about this topic in different ways?

Narrative (What happened)	Expository (What happens)	Argumentation (What should happen)
Memory driven: what happened in your life, and what did it mean to you?	Curiosity driven: what would other people want to know? What else would you want to find out?	Driven by the need for change: right/wrong, good/better, current ways/better ways
Ex: *The moment that we caught a marlin*	*All about* fishing tackle *How to catch* a marlin *Different kinds of* fishing trips *Background on* catch-and-release *Tips for* safe fishing	*Why* catch/release is important? *Why* families *should* fish together *Why* gulf waters *should* be protected *The value of* male bonding over fishing *The benefits of* spending time with your family out in nature ...
The time I broke my arm	All about compound fractures How to break your arm How to prevent from breaking your arm How to climb a tree correctly	Should parents pay more attention to their children? Why breaking your arm is a bad experience Why climbing a tree should be fun, not fatal

Figure 3–6 Barrett's elastic kernel sheet

Name Skylar

Elastic Kernel

Your topic: Roller coasters are fun

How could you write about this topic in different ways?

Narrative (What happened)	Expository (What happens)	Argumentation (What should happen)
Memory driven: what happened in your life, and what did it mean to you?	Curiosity driven: what would other people want to know? What else would you want to find out?	Driven by the need for change: right/wrong, good/better, current ways/better ways
Ex: *The moment that we caught a marlin*	*All about fishing tackle* *How to catch a marlin* *Different kinds of fishing trips* *Background on catch-and-release* *Tips for safe fishing*	*Why catch/release is important? Why families should fish together Why gulf waters should be protected The value of male bonding over fishing The benefits of spending time with your family out in nature ...*
When I went on the roller coaster	Superman: hero and roller coaster All About Roller Coasters How to have fun at a theme park the best roller coasters	Are roller coasters Safe? Why should you go to a theme park? What rides are the most fun at the theme park?

Figure 3–7 Skylar's elastic kernel sheet

Estefany wrote a personal narrative about an Easter egg hunt. After doing her elastic kernel activity, she chose the title "The Best Places to Hide Easter Eggs" as an informative article she'd like to write. She next chose the text structure "comparing notes" and completed her kernel essay, below. She is ready at this point to read it aloud to others, make any changes, and then design her details.

Name Estefany

Planning Sheet

Type of Writing (Check One)

☐ Writing about myself   ☐ Writing to inform me   ☑ Writing to inform others   ☐ Writing to persuade   ☐ Writing about literature

Put your **truism** (aka assertion aka problem aka main question) here

Best places to hide Easter Eggs

Put your **text structure** here. comparing notes (mine and others)

| Some people think | and other people think | But I think | what that tells me | | |

Write your **kernel essay** here.

1. They should put the eggs in plains sight
2. That they should be hidden so that they are really really hard to find
3. That eggs should not be in plain sight but also not the hardest thing to find
4. Depending on how old the finders are the challenge changes
5.
6.

Plan for **details**:

Action Detail
☐ snapshots   ☐ sensory details
☐ thoughtshots   ☐ ba-da-bing
☐ dialogue   ☐ _____

Infoshots
☐ description   ☐ synonyms/antonyms
☐ compare/contrast   ☐ part/whole
☐ cause/effect   ☐ item/category
☐ before/after   ☐ _____

Figure 3–8 Estefany's planning sheet

First, Yani wrote this personal narrative about her sister's experience having a baby. Then she did the elastic kernel essay and chose from her persuasive titles the article she'd most like to write, which follows.

It was the middle of the night when my sister called, the night before she was scheduled to get induced, having been days past her due date. Before my mom could tell me what Nikki had said, I already knew. She was in labor. I excitedly gathered the things I would need for the trip, and my mom and I left for Austin. I was beyond stoked, having had anticipated this moment for months.

The longer I was sitting there in the car, thoughts racing, my enthusiasm turned to anxiety. One main concern was whether or not we would make it to Austin in time. "Would we be too late and miss the whole thing? Would we not be there to comfort her when she needs us most?" More and more scary thoughts continued occupying my mind. Thinking of all the dreadful and potentially fatal, hypothetical situations, I started to cry. I was the epitome of worry. Then my sister called.

To my surprise, she sounded completely fine. It was regular Nikki talking on the phone, reassuring me that everything was going to be fine. With a considerable reduced amount of stress I continued the ride to the hospital with patience.

We arrived at the hospital, and made it to the room. Any amount of anxiety I still retained, left me when I saw my sister lying comfortably in her hospital bed encompassed by her husband, best friend, and a nurse. She greeted us looking like she always does, friendly. Her attitude made me feel like I had been overreacting to the whole situation by crying. However that was before we were made aware of the fact that she had received an epidural that wasn't set right. We learned this when she yelled in pain after having had suffered from an agonizing contraction. I knew that contractions were like period cramps times ten, so I assumed I had a somewhat understanding of what she was going through. It was like every time she experienced a contraction, I felt a sting myself. I wished so badly to switch places with her, in order to spare her from more pain.

It was nearly time for her to start pushing so the possibility to getting a working epidural was out of the question. This also means that my sister's best friend Donna, my mom, and I had to leave the room. My mom decided to spend her time waiting outside the hospital room while Donna and I made our way to the waiting room. My worry began to ensue. Donna helped calm me and waiting went by quick, with talking about things unrelated to my sister. It had been 30 minutes before Donna decided we should check on Nikki. The short walk to the room, I kept cool and didn't worry the least bit. That feeling changed when we arrived at the door, seeing my mom's own face carry the same worry I had earlier.

She explained quickly what happened with, "Nikki tore pretty badly . . . the doctor is stitching her up." I immediately started to cry. "This is what I was afraid of", I thought. The fact that could hear my sister letting out "ow's" through the opening in the door. Filled me with the familiar feeling of stinging.

Then I also saw through the crack in the door, my sister's baby laying red and crying in a strange plastic cart. I always imagined myself seeing Eisley for the first time and being in awe. But all I saw in that cart was a baby. It's strange to me now that I didn't feel anything when I first saw Eisley laying there. Seeing her for the first time played out much differently in my head, the countless number of times I imagined it. I'd never been in a situation like that before and was basing my expectations off of what I'd seen on 16 and Pregnant, television and movies.

Eisley is now three months old and I love her more than anything. Her smile, intentional or not, makes me happier than anyone else's could. I realized when it was all over that what my sister went through was worth it to have Eisley here. And I learned that you have to make sacrifices for the things you love.

—Yani Villanueva, grade 9

Here is Yani's persuasive piece, a result of her elastic kernel from the preceding personal narrative.

Is Natural Birth The Best Choice?

Some people think that natural birth is the best choice when having a baby. In case you have no idea what I'm talking about, I mean giving birth to a baby without an epidural. This is mostly because epidurals have the potential to affect labor and tend to cause side effects. My sister, for example, put in her birth plan that she wanted to have a natural birth. She didn't want to run the risk of the epidural having an effect on her baby. Though, when it came to the time she was in labor, she changed her mind, due to the pain from contractions. Although, it ended up not being set right, which is another risk women run if they choose to have an epidural.

Other people think that they won't be able to handle the pains of giving birth and being aware of their low tolerance for pain, they decide to receive an epidural. Since an epidural's effects are ambiguous, you can never be sure what might happen. What happens for one woman might not happen for the other, and that's why it's risky.

I personally, think that when the time comes for me to make this decision, I will choose to get an epidural. After witnessing my sister's labor, I decided that I would never want to endure that kind of pain. I honestly just don't think I'll be able to handle it. I wonder if I, like my sister, will change my mind when the day does come for me to make my decision.

—*Yani Villanueva, grade 9*

4 Mining Journals

If You Want to Start with Their Journal Writing

Basic Steps

1. Conduct journal hunt
2. Reveal categories
3. Choose papers that need to be written
4. Write them
   Choose structure
   Write a kernel essay

Tools

- "Journal Hunt" sheet
- Kernel essay planning sheet

Setting the Scene

Your students have been writing in their journals almost daily since school started. As you read their journals, you see how many subjects the students know about, are curious about, wish to change. If only, you think to yourself, we could figure out a way to get some of these topics into their expository writing assignments!

The Point

If you want to start with their journals, this journal hunt activity converts their freewriting into manageable topics, sorted into categories. It's a great way to draw out of them some of their expository conversations already underway.

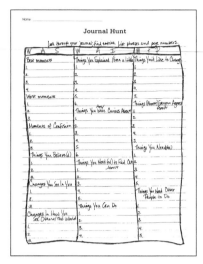

Figure 4–1 Journal hunt sheet

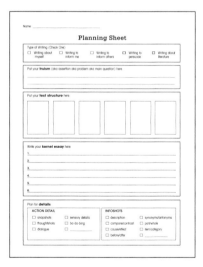

Figure 4–2 Planning sheet

Teaching It

- "Students, open your journals. First, we need to make sure the journal pages are numbered, like the pages in a book. If yours aren't numbered, number them now." *(Distribute the journal hunt sheets.)*

- "Look at the journal hunt sheet with me. You're going to look through your journals and find spots where you talked about any of these categories. Jot down on this sheet the page number and the topic you were talking about. Just see what you can find."

- "Tip: Don't write down any topics that you consider too private to share with other people."

(Allow the students plenty of time for this activity. It takes mine usually a whole forty-five-minute class period to complete the sheet.)

- "Now that you're finished, let's look at the top of the sheet. Do you see the initials at the tops of the columns? Fill in the words for each column. The first column is 'Writing About Self.' The second column is 'Writing About Information.' The third column is 'Writing to Persuade.'"

- "Now you have topics enough for a ton of essays!"

Debriefing

- "What surprises did you discover as you were filling out the sheet?"

- "What do you notice about your own trends in topics?"

- "Can you imagine what text structures you would use for full essays about any of these topics?"

What to Do Next

On a planning sheet:

Select a topic.

Select a structure.

Write a kernel essay.

Flesh it out with details.

Name: _____

Journal Hunt

Look through your journal; find entries. List phrases and page numbers.

W A S	W A I	W t P
Best moments	Things You Explained (Even a Little)	Things You'd Like to Change
1.	1.	1.
2.	2.	2.
3.	3.	3.
4.	4.	4.
Worst moments	5.	5.
1.	6.	Things (Almost) Everyone Agrees About
2.	Things You Are/Were Curious About	1.
3.	1.	2.
Moments of Confusion	2.	3.
1.	3.	4.
2.	4.	5.
3.	5.	Things You Need(ed)
Things You Believe(d)	6.	1.
1.	Things You Need (ed) to Find Out About	2.
2.	1.	3.
3.	2.	4.
Changes You See In You	3.	5.
1.	4.	Things You Need Other People to Do
2.	5.	1.
3.	Things You Can Do	2.
Changes In How You See Others/the World	1.	3.
	2.	4.
1.	3.	5.
2	4.	
3.		

Figure 4–3 Blank journal hunt sheet

Student Samples

Maggie filled out her journal hunt sheet. Notice the letters at the top of the columns? WAS, WAI, WTP. At this point you can direct students to fill in the missing letters to name the columns "Writing About Self," "Writing About Information," and "Writing to Persuade." Then they see what topics they have for those aims and use them for any appropriate assignments.

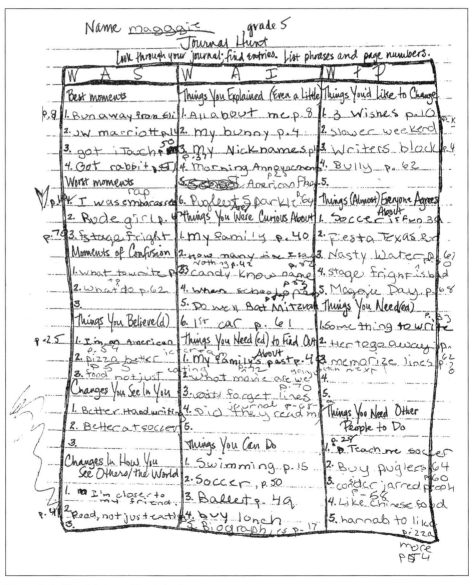

Figure 4–4 Maggie's journal hunt sheet

Maggie used one of her journal topics to write a kernel essay, fleshed out into the more detailed essay below.

Name __Maggie__

Planning Sheet

Type of Writing (Check One)

☐ Writing about myself   ☐ Writing to inform me   ☑ Writing to inform others   ☐ Writing to persuade   ☐ Writing about literature

Put your **truism** *(aka assertion aka problem aka main question) here*

I Admire my cousin Sophie.

Put your **text structure** *here.*

Giving An   Award

Who you choose	One, quality they have	One moment when that you saw that quality	How that moment affected you then	What you think of that person still	

Write your **kernel essay** *here.*

1. I admire my cousin, sophie.
2. She knows about nature.
3. One time we went around her property in the rain.
4. It made me feel Safe to Know I wasn't lost.
5. I think of her as a sister and not a cousin.
6.

Plan for **details**:

Action Detail

☐ snapshots   ☐ sensory details
☐ thoughtshots   ☐ ba-da-bing
☐ dialogue   ☐ _____

Infoshots

☐ description   ☐ synonyms/antonyms
☐ compare/contrast ☐ part/whole
☐ cause/effect   ☐ item/category
☐ before/after   ☐ _____

Figure 4–5 Maggie's planning sheet

Sophie

My cousin Sophie is ten years old, has short brown hair and green eyes. She was born in Seattle, Washington. She grew up in San Antonio and moved to Boerne when we were seven. Sophie is a part of my family who causes me happiness. She can be described as a nature lover.

Sophie knows a lot about nature. One time we went exploring around her property and saw different trees and animal bones. She pointed out all of them. I thought, she's very smart! Another time we were walking and she introduced me to all of the trees. One time we saw a puny rabbit and tried to catch it but it got away.

One time we went outside together in the rain. I didn't think I could survive the frigid weather. Sophie pointed at a little pond. We were sloshing in the rain when I took in the scenery of a small pond with small plants and brown water as nasty as sewer water. I thought, how deep is the water? I asked her that and she responded, "five feet deep."

It made me feel safe to know I wasn't lost! We were in the opposite of what I'm used to, almost like a different world.

Sophie is like a sister to me. We like to walk around and look at the trees and I think: Sophie and I are inseparable!

—Maggie Davis, grade 5

Ninth grader Christian filled out his journal hunt sheet and now has topics for dozens of essays or journal entries. It's also interesting to observe how the writing topics change as students grow older.

Name Christian

Journal Hunt

Look through your journal; find entries. List phrases and page numbers.

W A S	W A I	W † P
Best moments	Things You Explained (Even a Little)	Things You'd Like to Change
1. "Friends Ranch." Page 21	1. "Goosebumps." Page 59	1. "Straight A's." Page 19
2. "Basketball 10-11." P. 73	2. "water." Page 67	2. "Friend's Ranch." P. 21
3. "Macarthur." Page 63	3. "Fred." Page 69	3. "Drawing." Page 31
4. "Heat Game." Page 141	4. "Mumford and Sons." P. 113	4. "Basketball Loss." Page 37
Worst moments	5. "Cute little Bird." P. 47	5. "Zach." Page 85
1. "coach's Email." Page 35	6. "I'm Starving." Page 29	Things (Almost) Everyone Agrees About
2. "Last day." Page 61	Things You Were Curious About	1. "Football Lost." Page 37
3. "Worst." Page 131	1. "Lefty." Page 83	2. "Music." Page 103
Moments of Confusion	2. "Tap Zoo." Page 119	3. "TAKS." Page 129
1. "Grades." Page 19	3. "French." Page 43	4. "Mary Burk." Page 33
2. "Cute Little Bird." Page 47	4. "John David." Page 63	5. "Young Risers." Page 71
3. "Deadhead." Page 115	5. "Odysseus." Page 93	Things You Need(ed)
Things You Believe(d)	6. "Stronger." Page 143	1. "I'm starving." Page 29
1. "Football Victory." P. 57	Things You Need(ed) to Find Out About	2. "Basketball 10-11." P. 73
2. "Water." Page 67	1. "Boiller's Journal." Page 15	3. "Music." Page 103
3. "Fred." Page 69	2. "My Oldest Family Members." 45	4. "Stronger." Page 143
Changes You See In You	3. "Christmas Gifts." Page 79	5. "Stronger." Page 143
1. "Writing in Journal." 53	4. "Music." Page 103	Things You Want/Need Other People to Do
2. "Christmas." Page 97	5. "Grades." Page 105	
3. "Music." Page 103	Things You Can Do	1. "Macarthur." Page 61
Changes In How You See Others/ the World	1. "Centeral Catholic." Page 75	2. "Zach." Page 81
	2. "Football Victory." Page 57	3. "Fishing." Page 109
1. "Friend's Ranch." P. 39	3. "TAP Zoo." Page 119	4. "weights." Page 11
2. "Oscar." Page 87	4. "French." Page 43	5. "Grades." Page 105
3. "Brother." Page 107		

Figure 4–6 Christian's journal hunt sheet

Name Caroline

Journal Hunt

Look through your journal; find entries. List phrases and page numbers.

W A S	W A I	W + P
Best moments	**Things You Explained (Even a Little)**	**Things You'd Like to Change**
1. Cayman Islands pg.8	1. Symphony Ball is - pg18	1. War pg.130
2. beach pg14-15	2. Sophias birthday party pg41	2. learn peoples names! pg20
3. overalls pg32	3. Sister did for boyfreinds bday pg42	3. study more pg131
4. 80's workout pg35	4. Why not going to Jamaca pg49	4. The people who drink + drive pg.132-133
Worst moments	5. presentation pg132-133	5. My handwriting pg123
1. Math tests pg13-14	6. TAX test pg122-123	**Things (Almost) Everyone Agrees About**
2. Alex's Grandpa pg37	**Things You Were Curious About**	1. Polar Bear was fun! pg95
3. No homecoming date pg38	1. Home coming date? pg9	2. Biology tests are hard pg131
Moments of Confusion	2. What I'm doing after school? pg17	3. presentation was moving pg133
1. What to write? pg.9	3. Why watch highschool musical pg41	4. New Idea is cool pg123
2. Wheres my phone? pg15-16	4. Whats LA like? pg111	5. Tracks hard pg109
3. Who smeiled? pg36	5. Why you were holding a shoe? pg124	**Things You Need(ed)**
Things You Believe(d)	6. HOW I did on TAX? pg122-123	1. get in shape pg.106
1. family ADHD pg12	**Things You Need (ed) to Find Out**	2. a friend in ASC pg111
2. a christian pg12	1. If I go to a college About pg43	3. practice for TAX pg122-123
3. I have bad hand writing pg131	2. time goes by fast when waiting pg128	4. a book pg123
Changes You See In You	3. Country songs sad! pg113	5. to go to the LUG sleepover pg14-15
1. learned how to spell pg16	4. I am going to be soar from track pg109	**Things You Need Other People to Do**
2. Emilys not psyaho cause she didn't want to do pg120	5. drunk driving presentation pg133	1. My mom to let me go to Louisianna pg109
3. I like reading more than I used to pg23	**Things You Can Do**	2. Not to drink and drive pg133
Changes In How You See Others/The World	1. Sleep pg 415	3. My mom to buy a book pg123
1. see Aaron differently pg132-133	2. Track pg 106	4. Sarah to switch back to ASC pg111
2. Sarahs hair color pg108	3. dye hair pg108	5. Coach make track to be easier pg110
3. in highschool pg109	4. read pg123	

Figure 4–7 Caroline's journal hunt sheet

Here are some sample journal entries written by ninth graders. These are useful when students are struggling to complete the journal hunt sheet and saying, "I didn't write about any of these!" You can use these sample journal entries to model how to read a sentence or two and find slots for it on your hunt sheet.

march 8   #160
    I really wonder how planes work. I mean really how does that hunk of metal stay up in the sky without gravity just taking it down. Maybe its it jet that is super sonic and lifts it in the air. Maybe its wings that keep it steady in the air. I don't know, those are just my logical orservations. So I guess we are just to smart and know all the technology and short cuts to science. Putting up a huge, ton weighing plane with lots of people in it plus luggage. huh. Oviously it works.

March 2   #156
    Many people believe that aliens are not real. I believe they are. one reason I know this because scientist have found pictures and carvings of ancient people who are worshiping the sun, but the sun has something coming out from it. It looked like tiny ships beaming from it. Another reason I believe is because I recently looked up the Nazca lines. How are those giant drawings made and are big enough to see from the sky? Also I saw that the Nazca people band their infants head to make them longer, this is said to be done to worship their god.

human skull →   alien →

TEACHER TALK: Having trouble finding anything for your hunt sheet? Let me read one with you. *I really wonder how planes work . . .* that's something you are curious about, right? That could go right on the sheet. Maybe that's a change in how you see the world, too, about how we know so many *shortcuts to science*?

Let's look at your next entry. *Many people believe that aliens are not real.* That could go on the sheet in "things almost everyone agrees about," right? *I believe they are.* That's something you believe, for "things you believe." Then you explain it, so that's "things you explained." See that? You have already filled in five spots on the hunt sheet from these two journal entries alone.

Figure 4–8 Ashley's journal entries

These sample journal entries can also be used to model filling out the hunt sheet.

9/15/11

TEACHER TALK: *Let's see . . . today we went to the library, okay . . . I really like being there because I think it's really cool . . . right there! That's something you explained, even a little. You can put that right on the hunt sheet under "things you explained." And how about "things you can do"? Finding where types of books are . . . is that something you need to find out about? Or something you can do now? You can fill that into your sheet right there.*

Today we went to the library. I really liked being there because I think it really cool to see all the different varieties of books & thing. I got to sit in the couch chair and it was very comfortable. We did a scavenger hunt in the library today. We had to go around the library finding where types of books are and where all of the things were located. The top 3 that finished first got candy bags. Robin, Will and Dylan were the first three people to finish. It really didn't matter because in the end everyone ended up getting candy.

—*Ben McSween*

9/20/11

TEACHER TALK: *What's a running clock game? Oh, you explained it right here . . . you could write that down as something you explained. How about something you'd like to change? You'd like to change the running clock game. Check your last line. A moment of confusion. You filled in three spots on your hunt sheet with this one entry alone!*

I just found out that our district game this Thursday that was supposed to be away now is home and so is JV so that means that we have 4 games all on the same field and so we will have a running clock game. That means that all the games will have the clocks not stopped the entire time. So each game I think has 9 minute quarters and so each team will be 36 minutes to about 45 if you include halftime. I really hope this isn't true because that would suck. The game would literally fly by. But still with all of that going on I think the last game won't end until like 10ish.

I'm confused about what's going to happen.

—*Robert Schuler*

5 11-Minute Essay

If You Want
a Quick Backup Plan
for Anxiety Reduction

Basic Steps

1. Adopt or revise truism
2. Conduct guided writing using "11-minute essay" structure
3. Share
4. Repeat until internalized

Tools

- 11-minute essay structure and instructions
- Visual Writing Prompts from the Heinemann website (go to www.heinemann.com/products/04239.aspx and click on Companion Resources)

Setting the Scene

You don't really know where to start with expository writing, and you're worried. You'd really like to have one surefire plan that students can use as a fallback habit for any situation.

The Point

This structure is like mental gymnastics. Students take a prompt and find evidence of it in several different settings outside their own personal experience. They learn to quickly switch gears mentally, and with a little practice, they are able to build their ability to connect thoughts to themselves, to literature, and to their world. In this short guided-writing exercise, students expand on an opinion and a piece of artwork. This synthesizes their experience from literature and life.

Teaching It

(On an overhead projector or document camera, place a piece of artwork with a truism that correlates with a piece of literature you are reading in class. This guided writing will take eleven minutes.)

4. Sometimes good things don't last very long.

A veces las cosas buenas no duran mucho tiempo.

Figure 5–1 This is an example of a visual writing prompt.

"Look at the artwork."

"Think about this sentence underneath as I read it to you. Do you think it's true? Copy the sentence, the truism, onto your paper."

"For the next minute, explain the statement. What does it mean? What is your interpretation of it?" *(Give the students one minute, and then ask them to finish up their thought and stop writing.)*

"Take a breath and indent. Think about all of the stories you've read, all the books. Look at the first sentence you wrote. Now think about the stories you've read until you think of one that shows you how true this sentence (your first sentence) is. Indent, and tell what story you thought of, and how it shows that this sentence is true." *(Give the students three minutes, and then ask them to finish up their thought and stop writing.)*

"Take a breath and indent. Think about all of the movies you've ever seen. Look at the first sentence you wrote. Now think about the movies you've seen until you think of one that shows you how true this sentence (your first sentence) is. Indent, and tell what movie you thought of, and how it shows that this sentence is true." *(Give the students three minutes, and then ask them to finish up their thought and stop writing.)*

"Take a breath and indent. Think about all of the history you've ever learned. You've learned the history of the world, of our country, of recent times, of ancient times. Look at the first sentence you wrote. Now think about moments in history until you think of one that shows you how true this sentence (your first sentence) is. Indent, and tell what moment in history you thought of, and how it shows that this sentence is true." *(Give the students three minutes, and then ask them to finish up their thought and stop writing.)*

"Take a breath and indent one more time. In the next minute, finish with something your discussion leaves you wondering about the statement. Reread what you've written, and begin your last paragraph with the words 'All this makes me wonder . . .' or 'I wonder . . .'" *(Give the students one minute, and then ask them to finish up their thought and stop writing.)*

Debriefing

- "Was one of the connections more difficult than the others?"
- "Do you think one of the parts of your paper is weaker than the others? Delete it!"
- "What would you need to add to help the paragraphs move from one to the next?"
- "Is this the only way to structure an essay?"

What to Do Next

- Draw the text structure on the board as a visual.
- Share a few volunteers, or partner share. Put the pieces away.
- In several of the following days, repeat the exercise with different visuals and truisms. Repeat the process.

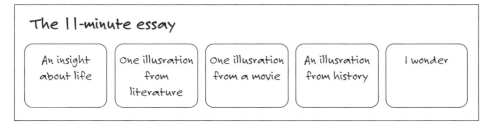

The 11-minute essay

| An insight about life | One illusration from literature | One illusration from a movie | An illusration from history | I wonder |

Fig. 5–2 11-minute essay text structure

TEACHER TALK: The structure previously known as "The Insight Garden" has, through time, been nicknamed the "11-Minute Essay." It first appeared in Barry Lane and Gretchen Bernabei's book, *Why We Must Run with Scissors: Voice Lessons in Persuasive Writing (2001).*

Student Samples

Many prompts are set up using this three-step process: step 1 is a photo or text to read; step 2 is a related truism; step 3 is the actual prompt.

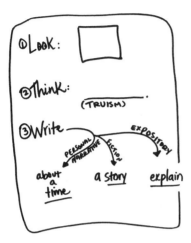

Fig. 5–3 Look Think Write chart

Here is an example of an 11-minute essay written by a fourth grader.

Friendship

I believe that no matter what path you take you will always come to a true friend even if it takes your hole life.

I know this is true because I read a book called *Dolphin Tale*. When I read that book my eyes turned into a water fall because I learned about true friendship. Also how nothing can come in between real friends because the boy would do anything to prevent Winter the Dolphin from dieing. I knew that if Winter died it would be like braking a hart in half. So true friendship is what the boy did.

I know true friendship is true because I saw a movie called *Polar Express* the girl and boy cared about the other boy that when he tried to get on the train that the boy stopped the train. They also went with him so he wouldn't feel lonely. The looked after him when the back of the train came off. I believe that shows true friendship.

I feel that this true because when I moved from my old home I lost my friend but as I moved on I found new friends.

But I wonder if I will find more friends?

—Diana Colunga, grade 4

This 11-minute essay was written by a sixth grader. Clearly some transitional work and details would strengthen the overall essay, but for eleven minutes, it shows strong core understanding, multiple connections to work with, and striking insight.

Happy Moments to Bad Moments

Sometimes good things don't last very long. Sometime fun or happy things might only last for a small moment.

In *Hunger Games*, by Suzzane Collins, Katniss is happy with what she has in district twelve. But, then she goes to the Hunger games. She wasn't happy any more.

In the movie *We are Marshall*, the team is coming back from a win in another state, when the plane they are in crashes. The whole team dies and the good moment is replaced by a very bad moment.

A long time ago, Abraham Lincoln abolished slavery. African American people were happy because they would be treated fairly, as they should. But that happy moment ended quickly when Abraham Lincoln was assassinated.

I wonder why people or people's things have to ruin a good moment and turn it into a bad, sad, or painful moment.

—*Phillip Kaplan, grade 6*

In this 11-minute essay, the writer finds an unusual perspective in his take on "treasures."

Treasures for Life

The treasures in our lives are often hidden. What this line means is that gifts that G-d gives to the Earth can be very hard to find.

In the book *Holes* Stanley has to go to a facility. There he finds a hidden treasure that was there for a long time, who changed his life so a bad thing was good. This treasure was his new friend.

In the movie Jack and Jill, Jack doesn't realize that his sister is a gift from G-d so he's mean to her until he realizes that some people don't have siblings. He didn't see his treasure until then.

One moment in history is Columbus finding North America. No one did that before him, so it was a hidden part of this Earth.

I wonder why treasures are so hard to find. Why can't they just come right to us?

—*Joseph Klein, grade 7*

This author has taken her 11-minute essay and expanded the connections with further explanation and details.

Falling Stinks

When you fall, you fall hard. It happens. Just get up and pretend it never did. A person very important in my life taught me this. I have known him all my life. He is my father. My dad has helped me through the best and worst times. No matter where he is in the world, he's always been there for me. I think that what he was trying to teach me are these following words. You're going to fall. Don't regret it, it's not your fault. Just get up and keep on walking. If and when you do fall, be strong and keep on going. Don't let anyone put you down. Just because someone does something to you doesn't mean that you have to make it hurt.

A book that I know that shows this is "Night World" the first book in the series. A girl named Rashel Jordan is the main character. She was five years old when her mother and brother were killed right in front of her by a vampire. The book skips to when she was seventeen. She became a vampire hunter, and the most famous one at that. She ended up figuring out who the person was that killed her mother and brother. His name was Hunter Redfern. Rashel ended up killing him. She spent her whole life doing nothing but hunting for the killer and won the battle. She accomplished what she worked so hard for doing. She got up and kept walking. Rashel Jordan was strong and kept on going no matter what. She didn't let one person (or should I say vampire) ruin her life. She even got her brother back since he wasn't really dead. Hunter Redfern changed him into a vampire. Rashel tried so hard doing one thing so she got two things back in return. She got her revenge and her brother. Even though he was changed, she got him back for trying so hard.

Rashel wasn't the only one who had to get up after falling. "The Notebook," is about a guy named Noah Calhoun whom has a summer romance with a girl named Allie Hamilton. Her parents didn't like Noah and made her leave her summer fun early. Noah had lost his one true love. A couple years later, Noah had bought a house and it was in the paper since it was a mansion. Allie was getting married in a few weeks when she saw the paper with him in it. So, she went to his house and they fell in love, again. They got married and had kids. She ended up having Alzheimer's disease. Every day she would forget who he was, who she was, and were she was. Every day in the morning Noah would go to Allie's room and read her his diary (or notebook) from when they met till when she had to make the choice to choose him or her fiance. One night she remembered who he was. They fell asleep in the same bed and died in the middle of the night. They were very old and stayed at a retirement that takes care of in need old people. Noah never gave up when she had to leave him. He never gave up when he found out she had a fiance. He got up and kept on walking. Noah got Allie back, because he had faith and pretended it never happened. He didn't let her parents put him down. He loved her that much.

I used to play soccer in California. I have played soccer since I was 4 years old. I was at a soccer game on the weekend. I was sunny and warm. I was pretty fast for my age and knew a few foot skills. There was a really tall and heavyset girl. She rammed into me and I somersaulted in the air. I landed on my back. Everyone was wondering if I was okay. The expressions on their faces were priceless. Mainly shocked or faces of concern. I didn't even know that I fell until I realized that I was on the ground. I got up and ran after the ball. I ended up scoring a goal. I got up and kept walking (or running in my case). I didn't let one girl ruin my chance. When you fall, you fall hard. It happens. Just get up and pretend it never did. That's the way that I'm going to live.

—*Katie James, grade 9*

Even though the best people may have flaws, it's their perfections you should concentrate. The best people may have that one flaw that you always notice, and you can bother them about it and possibly lose them as a friend, or you can concentrate on their perfections and make a good friend.

In "One Step Ahead" Detective Wallander knows that Kalle has some imperfections, but instead of bugging him about it he congratulates him for being such a good cop. Even though Wallander doesn't know it until Kalle is dead, Kalle considered Detective Wallander his best friend, and even though Wallander didn't think of Kalle in the same way, it meant a lot to him.

In "Gone in 60 Seconds" Memphis Raines is an ex-car thief. He gets back into stealing cars because his brother will be killed if he doesn't deliver all the cars he's supposed to. Memphis is willing to put his life on the line to help his brother, who put himself in this predicament. When people watch this movie they don't think of how bad a person Memphis is because he steals car, they think, "Wow, this is one great guy willing to put his life on the line to deliver enough cars to save his brother, Kip."

Tristan Griffith is a really good friend of mine who I met in Ricardo, Texas. He sometimes took over a conversation and wrote really long essays that when read, would take up the entire class. He also was one of the most kind and determined people I have ever met. I have never forgotten the time when we had a football game and he showed up to play even though he had crushed his toe by dropping a steel tractor part on it. I think I was just about the only other person apart from his family who knew about this because he never once complained. The day before the game he shoved that toe, which was about half the size of his entire foot, inside his cleats and was our starting runner-back. He is just one of those people who you are never bored around, even in some of the most boring conditions, because he finds ways to have fun and make your time worthwhile.

I have always wondered how some people seem to have an urge to find someone's imperfections, and not their perfections. The world would be a much better place if people actually tried to make people feel good about themselves.

—*Ale Braun, grade 9*

This 11-minute essay was written by a teacher. She repeats one of the opening images in the ending, and creates a powerful metaphor. This framing would make a great craft lesson for students to notice and imitate.

Sometimes good things don't last very long. Good things can be tangible, like a sticky, melting chocolate ice cream cone enjoyed at the end of a hot summer. Sometimes, it can be a feeling like the pitter-pat of your heart when you are near your first love, but just as lovely as a summer treat.

In *Romeo and Juliet,* their whirlwind, star-crossed romance was as short lived as Billy Ray's "Achy Breaky Heart." The two lovers shared a passionate, sweet love hidden beneath balconies and behind shadows. Too soon, the young sweethearts love is sealed with an untimely death.

Two clandestine lovers, the poet Christian and courtesan Satine, share a brief amorous affair before Satine is overcome by an illness only to die in her poet's arms. But not before the characters in Moulin Rouge are able to create a beautiful memory.

In Roman times, though the Empire lasted approximately 200 years, they had only just begun to explore important academic and philosophical issues. For the budding society, their time was cut short, much like Romeo and Juliet and Christian and Satine, never to live again. All cut short before their time.

I wonder if, within the constraints of time and mortality, good things can last beyond a season or are we an ice cream cone beneath the blazing sun?

—*Chandra Malone Garrett, teacher*

6

Inner Streams/ Gritty Life

If You Want Them to Explore Topics for Deep Development and Systemic Growth

Basic Steps

1. Create gritty life quick list
2. Kernel essay #1 (write/share)
3. Kernel essay #2 (write/share)
4. Kernel essay #3 (write/share)
5. Choose one
6. Add details

Tools

- Gritty life quick list
- Kernel essay planning sheet (in appendix)
- Text structure choices (see pages 145–165)

GRITTY LIFE QUICK LIST

pet peeves
1. interrupting
2. bullies in authority

shopping list
3. duct tape
4. strawberries

topics of conversation
5. Charlie Boggess's brother
6. Julian's
7. crystals in the window
8. piñata buster painting

things I own
things I can do
9. whistle up a taxi
10. sing one Japanese song

news
11. Arab Spring
12. Occupy Wall St. protests

Setting the Scene

It's probably early in the year. You'd like to explore what thoughts the students may be having, without directing them too much, and to show them that they can easily take their own swirling, shapeless thoughts and sculpt them into wonderfully organized and coherent essays.

Figure 6–1 Gritty life quick list sample

The Point

For informative writing assignments, teachers have traditionally turned to units and pre-written topics. James Moffett (1968) says that we should use students' ideas, and not just their memories, as raw material for all kinds of academic work. But how do we capture the background thoughts they walk in with? This exercise helps to mine those topics, topics that are more like the grit in our lives, topics that can be useful for any kind of expository writing.

(Students will need paper in front of them, or they can make this list in the backs of their journals, in their writing folders, wherever it makes sense to keep a list of topics.)

- "Do you ever have a hard time thinking up something to write about?"

Fig. 6–2 Pet Peeve text structure

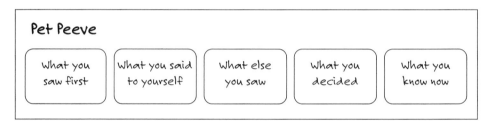

- "Think about this: when a conversation is over, it's not really over, is it? You might walk away from it, but your brain keeps it going, and you replay the conversation, imagining what else the other person would say, what else you would say, revising it, continuing it. That happens with all of your conversations. When you walk into this classroom, your brain is operating dozens of mental conversations at once. Those are a gold mine for writing topics. Today we're going to do some digging for topics."
- "Number your papers 1 to 12."
- "For numbers 1 and 2, do you have any pet peeves? When people do these things, it makes you growl. Maybe they happen at home or school, or maybe at the grocery store, in the car, at the movies, anywhere. List two."
- "For numbers 3 and 4, what's on your shopping list? Name two items that you need to buy at the grocery store or any other kind of store."
- "For numbers 5 and 6, think back through the last couple of weeks. Think about all the conversations you have had with your friends or with family. List two topics of conversation, two things you have talked about with your friends or family in the last couple of weeks."
- "For numbers 7 and 8, think about the things you own. Some are treasures, and some are just stuff. List two things you own that you're glad are yours."
- "For 9 and 10, consider this: when you were born, you weren't able to do very much. Since then, you have learned to do many things. List two things you can do, things that you can do well now."

- "For 11 and 12, think about all the things that have been in the news. These could be about sports, about our city or state, about the world. List two topics that have been in the news."
- "This is your gritty life quick list. You can write about any of the topics here, and we will use some of them, too."

Debriefing

- "Which topics were the easiest to think of?"
- "Which topics were most difficult?"

(Compare student responses to make the point that nothing works equally well for all writers, that we all need choices so that we can use what works best for us.)

Resources

James Moffett's *Teaching the Universe of Discourse*

What to Do Next

- Select one of the topics.
- Guide students through a kernel essay, using the text structure for that topic.
- Have students share aloud in groups.
- Put the kernel essays aside.
- Repeat this process on subsequent days, until students have several kernel essays that they have shared with peers.
- Have students select their favorite kernel essay and flesh it out with details. (*Use infoshots or the text icons chart for a variety of details.*)

Spin-offs

- Instead of using all of the topics in the same class period, you can use them one at a time, in greater depth. For ideas, see "Gritty life quick list, detailed," next, to spend more time on each. You could make a Friday list for Monday writing, on each of these detailed categories.
- For more variety, try changing any words in the questions. Or insert the word *not* into any of the questions (one thing you can *not* do well, one thing that's *not* on your shopping list).
- To include literature, you could have students write these lists from a point of view of a literary character (e.g., Charlotte's pet peeves, Wilbur's favorite possession, Templeton's shopping list).

Gritty Life Quick List, Detailed

PET PEEVES	SHOPPING LIST	CONVERSATIONS	PRIZED POSSESSIONS	COMPETENCY	NEWS/GOSSIP	MEMORY
Things that people do that bother you	*Things you need to buy or replace*	*What you have talked about*	*Things you own in your*	*Something you can do*	*Things you know about from world news*	*Moments*
▪ at home ▪ at school ▪ in the car ▪ at the movies ▪ in restaurants ▪ at a store	▪ food you don't want to run out of ▪ clothing items you need to replace ▪ must-have items ▪ electronics that have changed your life	▪ with family ▪ with a friend ▪ in the last 2 days ▪ on the phone ▪ during a meal ▪ in email ▪ on your way somewhere	▪ living room ▪ kitchen ▪ bedroom ▪ yard ▪ garage ▪ car *Things you've found* *Things you've lost* *Things you wish for* *Things you remember*	▪ noises you can make ▪ arts/drawings you know how to do ▪ things you can say in another language ▪ songs/poems you can perform ▪ athletic (specific) feats you've learned to do *Things related to* ▪ games ▪ food prep ▪ comm skills ▪ other skills ▪ secret skills ▪ hidden skills _____ _____	▪ current events ▪ neighborhood talk ▪ American news ▪ sports news ▪ citizen movements ▪ recent headlines ▪ recent countries in conflict ▪ recent disasters ▪ people in the news	▪ when you felt proud of someone else ▪ involving a struggle ▪ you wish you were on video ▪ you wish you had a snapshot of ▪ reptile moment ▪ bird moment ▪ insect moment ▪ hair moment ▪ clothing moment ▪ shoes moment ▪ with an animal ▪ during a holiday ▪ moment you want to remember

Figure 6–3 Gritty life quick list, detailed

One Kernel, So Many Spin-off Lessons

Consider this kernel essay, using the pet peeve structure:

1. *I was trying to enter the freeway on a warm, crowded day, and behind me was a black souped-up Mustang sitting on my bumper.*
2. *Gee, I thought, what is this guy's problem?*
3. *About that time he zoomed around me barely missing my bumper.*
4. *Why can't there be a rule that men are banned from driving on the freeway?*
5. *Men are rude. Why can't men drivers be polite and courteous?*

—Jennifer B. Ferguson, teacher

When asked "If your students produced something like this in class, what would you do next? How would you use this?" a group of teachers in Katy, Texas, knew what they might do with it next:

They said . . .

- Add it to the students' writing folders under "ideas."
- Develop into a personal narrative concerning a time I felt justified.
- Write conversational narratives for writing dialogue.
- Turn this into a rough draft. Then share and fill in the missing pieces.
- Shape it into informative writing:
  - What makes people mad
  - Ways people can be selfish
  - How to avoid a fight
  - News article about an incident
- Turn into compare and contrast, using different situations or different people at different times.
- Use the questions from kernel essays to help students develop anecdotes, short stories used to make a point, which they can then use as a part of a narrative essay, introduction to a persuasive essay, or introduction to an expository topic.
- Introduce a story about a relationship with the person who caused the pet peeve.

- Use it as a good lead for a persuasive essay, with students giving opposing sides:
  - Letter to the editor, on using your blinker when driving
  - Editorial writing
- Make a great testimonial. I could see this used as a "what not to do" writing, too. Not so much for the actions of others but for your response to the situation.
- Turn this into a great public service announcement, including technology; make a trailer, possibly lead to research writing.
- Turn it around and advocate it.
- Teach word choice by drawing a scale for a continuum of words, from slightly annoyed to irate!
- Take your #1 sentence and come up with a how-to paper.
- Take your #4 sentence to do a persuasive paper.
- Use it to introduce the concepts of tone and voice.
- Write it both with a serious tone and with a humorous tone.
- Demonstrate how one topic can become informative, persuasive, anything.
- Use it at the beginning of the year to get to know the students.

Sample kernel essays, using the text structure "prized possession":

> I just couldn't do without my camera.
> It is the most super thing that I can use. It captures moments I might not remember.
> It has a place that you can see how many pictures that are left.
> Before I had it I was incomplete.
> That's why I need it.
> Without it I would not have a very great memory and I wouldn't know much about my family.
>
> —S. Ransdell, grade 6

> I just couldn't do without my dog, Max.
> He is the most important thing that I love the most.
> It has black and white dots.
> Before I had it I was scared to sleep by myself.
> That's why I like him.
> Without it I would be scared.
>
> —Riana, grade 6

I just couldn't do anything without my glasses.

It is the most important thing that I have. Without them I couldn't see well at all.

It has lenses that make me see clearly.

Before I had it I was miserable. I couldn't see.

That's why I need glasses which I have now.

Without it I have the worst eyes in the world.

—*Bryce, grade 6*

Example kernel essays written by teachers:

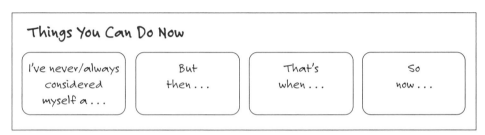

Things You Can Do Now

| I've never/always considered myself a . . . | But then . . . | That's when . . . | So now . . . |

Figure 6–4
Things You Can Do Now text structure

I never considered myself a cloud reader. But then, I grew up watching and learning from my grandfather, a 4th grade-educated sharecropper. That's when I learned to look at the clouds and what is over, under, beside, and beyond them in addition to shape, color, texture, and density. So now I can look at the clouds and exactly predict the weather in Texas.

—*Marla Goldfader, teacher*

I've never considered myself very ethnic or intriguing. I grew up in Texas to a Caucasian family without any exciting recipes. But then I decided to try some ethnic foods and recipes. That's when I tried lasagna for the first time. I mean real lasagna with homemade bolognese and fresh basil. So now when I want to feel intriguing, accomplished, I'll try a new recipe. Even if I am just a plain old white girl.

—*Lindsay E. Askins, teacher*

Figure 6–5
Shopping List text
structure

I need to buy Deacon's 4ᵗʰ birthday cake. Without it, Deacon's party will not be
super. This causes me mixed emotions. Eventually, Deacon will not need birthday cakes. And so I'd better savor this time with my boys because they won't
be little forever. I only hope Deacon always remembers how much we love him.

—*Margo Faulkner, teacher*

I need to buy strawberries.
Without it, I'll have to eat the icky ones rotting in the fridge.
This causes me to gag.
Eventually, I'll have to go to Randall's anyway.
And so, I'll do this on the way home from here.
I only hope I can get out of Randall's without the chips, dip, chocolate bars and
M&Ms I really want.

—*Jennifer Gwydir, teacher*

*The following kernel essays show the startlingly broad range of content that
students and teachers will use to fill in the same kernel.*

Figure 6–6
One Thing . . .
Talk About text
structure

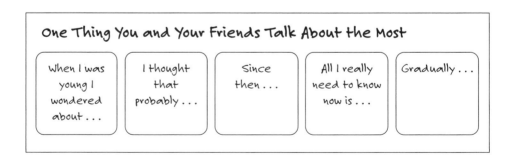

How Things Are Going

When I was young I wondered about what my brother was doing.

I thought that probably he was either doing push-ups or in class somewhere.

Since then, I learned that though he's at the military academy, he's not always working out or doing drills.

All I really need to know now is, is he really doing OK like he says he is?

Eventually I will get to call him again and he'll tell me what's going on up there and I'll tell him what happens here.

—Cameron Young, grade 6

Gossip

When I was young I wondered about the vicous words coming out of adults mouths.

I thought that probably adults were talking about a brutal person.

Since then, I've tried to keep my slender mouth shut, avoiding argumants.

All I really need to know now is how comments trigger brains to stop the problem.

Eventually, I will stop the madness, leaving our many raced world at peace.

—Leggy Q., grade 6

Allergies

When I was young, I wondered about being allergic to everything and what that would be like.

I thought that probably no one was allergic to everything.

Since then, I have discovered that I am allergic to pollen.

All I really need to know now is, if I am allergic to kiwi, one of my favorite fruits.

Eventually, I will find out if I am allergic to kiwi.

—Lizzie Barry, grade 6

Mansions in India

(I read this in Ripley's Believe It or Not)

When I was young I wondered about rich people.

I thought that probably they could have anything they wanted.

Since then, I have realized it takes work to earn money.

All I really need to know now is how a single man could make a billion doller house in India.

Eventually, I will visit India to learn about their lifestyle and the type of jobs they have that would give a man a billion dollars for a house.

—*Abbey Williams, grade 6*

Lurking in the Dark

When I was young, I wondered about creatures lurking in the dark.
I thought that probably they would eat me.
Since then, I have *SOMEWHAT* overcome that fear.
All I really need to know now is, where do they hide?
Eventually, I will find their hideout.

—*Mattie Vasquez, grade 6*

Female Discrimination

When I was young I wondered about why most stay at home parents were female.
I thought that probably it was just their job.

Since then, I've realized that it's not their "job" but it's something that's been drilled into them and made a stereotype over the past centuries.

All I really need to know now is that I am just as equal as the next person, and should have equal opportunities.

Eventually I will hope to instill that we are all equal, and should not be deprived or discriminated against because of our gender.

—*Demar Gunter, grade 6*

When I was young, I wondered about where my mom was taking us for dinner.

I thought that probably, the food there would be really good.

Since then, it always reaches my mind: Where or what we are eating for dinner.

All I really need to know now is, what food they serve there. Is it good?

Eventually I will make the decisions for dinner, but for now, that's my mom's job.

—*Eliana Bennington, grade 6*

When I was young, I wondered about how men and women stayed together for more than 25 years. I thought that probably only the really "nice" and spiritually good people stayed together. Since then I have discovered that patient people, human doormats, frozen-emoticon bodies, or saints can create a long-term relationship. All I really need to know now is how to keep my spouse alive and viable for 30 more years. Gradually, God will show me the tools I need to spare with my spouse and grant me a fresh peppering of patience.

—*Jo Rose, teacher*

When I was young I would wander about the yard looking for things to put in my fairy garden. It was not really my fairy garden. It was the fairy's fairy garden. I was just working on it. I thought that probably the fairies came out only at night because I had never really seen one. I say "really seen" one because I had seen things that may have been fairies. Since then I do not need proof of the fairies. I know they exist. All I really need to know now is where is the best place to get my fairy garden supplies. Gradually, I stopped making fairy gardens but not before I taught my daughter how to make one.

—*Toni Gloria Canestaro, teacher*

When I was young I wondered about what it would be like to live somewhere else other than my hometown of Beeville. I thought that probably living somewhere else where the weather, people, and outdoor activities would be different. Since then, I've learned that although things are different out there, it's always the same—I would be there. All I need to know now is how to look in my own backyard with new, interesting and creative eyes. Gradually, I began to transform things where I lived starting with my office, then on to the other parts of my house.

—*Sylvia Vasquez, teacher*

This fully detailed piece was written first as a kernel essay and then detailed by the author, a teacher. He posted it on his blog about using technology in the classroom.

Seeking the White Hart

When I was young, I wondered about the White Hart, that mythical creature sent by the gods to the brave hunter on a quest for something more. I encountered the White Hart story in many a tale, a creature hovering at the edge of vision, a heartbeat from despair and failure. *Clay Burell seeks the White Hart,* which he characterizes like this:

> My hard drive has dozens and dozens of carefully selected ebooks about my areas of interest right now—primarily World History and Chinese History. I've invested a good bit of cash into this because I want a "searchable academic library" on my laptop, out of the following heretical conviction: academic ebooks on a hard drive are a better resource than the internet . . . it would be *even more magical if my hard drive search results looked more like Google's, and less like Mac's.*

I thought that probably I could be the hunter on a journey to save his people (in this case, a fellow edublogger), seeking out the divine wisdom (Google), with only my strength, wits, and the mercy from above (search engine results) to find that which the people need.

Since then, since I began my search, I've begun to despair that what I've found is truly worthwhile. What if the solution I've found isn't the right one? Perhaps, it is merely an illusion, a false trail laid by no one, and I've wasted precious moments down the wrong trail to a box canyon? What if *Google Quick Search* isn't the right answer? When I installed *Google Quick Search* on my Mac running OS X.6 Leopard, it gave me these results when I searched on Moodle, the start of many a PDF document on my machine:

All I really need to know now is if this is the solution that Clay had in mind when he began searching. Gradually, I hope that desktop search tools will become better integrated and the tools work well.

—*Miguel Guhlin, teacher*

7

Prompt Assignments

If You Want Them
to Respond to a Prompt
for Fast Habit Development

Basic Steps

1. Assignment prompt and three to five structures
2. Kernel essay (write/share)
3. Flesh out with details

Tools

- Text structure choices (in Glossary of Terms)
- Expository prompts
- Kernel essay planning sheet (in appendix)
- Text Icon glossary
- Ba-da-bing instructions (in Glossary of Terms)

Setting the Scene

You might be fretting. On the one hand, you're all for allowing students to create their own topics and thoughts. That helps them grow and discover their own thoughts and identities. On the other hand, you'd like them to be able to respond on demand to a prompt from someone else. They'll have to perform in this way on the SAT writing test, on their college essays, and even possibly much sooner, on a state assessment. You're pretty sure that benchmarking isn't the same as instructing, so you'd like to give them some instruction, some shaping for this kind of performance.

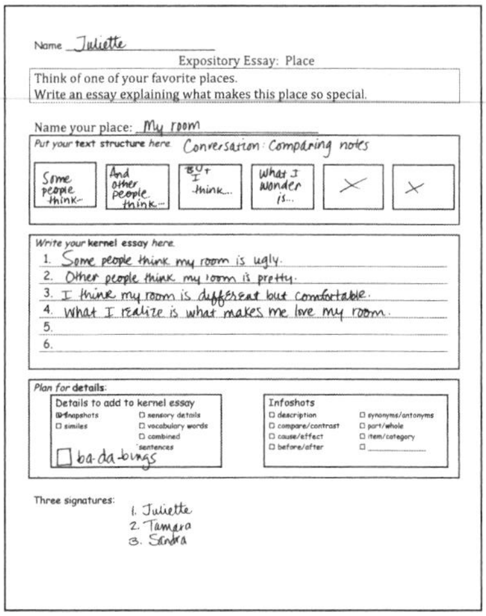
Name Juliette

Expository Essay: Place

Think of one of your favorite places.
Write an essay explaining what makes this place so special.

Name your place: My room

Put your text structure here Conversation: Comparing notes

Some people think…	And other people think…	But I think…	What I wonder is…	X	X

Write your kernel essay here

1. Some people think my room is ugly.
2. Other people think my room is pretty.
3. I think my room is different but comfortable.
4. What I realize is what makes me love my room.
5.
6.

Plan for details:

Details to add to kernel essay
- ☑ snapshots
- ☐ similes
- ☐ sensory details
- ☐ vocabulary words
- ☐ combined sentences
- ☐ ba-da-bings

Infoshots
- ☐ description
- ☐ compare/contrast
- ☐ cause/effect
- ☐ before/after
- ☐ synonyms/antonyms
- ☐ part/whole
- ☐ item/category
- ☐ ______

Three signatures:
1. Juliette
2. Tamara
3. Sandra

Figure 7–1 Juliette's planning sheet

The Point

Expository writing asks students to explain their thinking about persons, places, things, concepts, and opinions. Setting up tasks for these can give them practice with lots of support at the beginning when they need it.

Teaching It

(You can select one of the prompts, customize the kernel essay planning sheet template, or download a template from the Companion Resources at www.heinemann.com/products/04239.aspx, or adapt your own.)

- "Students, here is an essay assignment for you. Let's read the prompt together." (Do.) "You may use any of the structures on the back of the assignment sheet, and first you'll write a kernel essay. What's a kernel essay?"
- "You write one sentence for each box in the structure. Would you like to see an example before you begin?" (Show them one if they ask.)
- (Post a due date for a kernel essay and a due date for the finished, detailed essay. Make sure to show them a rubric ahead of time and give them a word count range for their finished piece.)

Debriefing

- "While we were sharing, which kinds of details did you think were the most effective?"
- "Can we use ba-da-bings in expository writing?"

Bank of Expository Prompts

In each of the following, the word *explain* signals an expository (not narrative) essay. You could change any of the content words in the prompts, especially the adjectives, to create many more prompts.

Who is the most surprising person you know? Write an essay about that person, explaining what makes him or her so surprising.

Who is the most helpful person you know? Write an essay about that person, explaining what makes him or her so helpful.

Who is the most focused person you know? Write an essay about that person, explaining what makes him or her so focused.

Who is the funniest person you know? Write an essay about that person, explaining what makes him or her so funny.

Where is the place you consider the most exciting? Write an essay about that place, explaining what makes it so exciting.

Where is a place you consider the most peaceful? Write an essay about that place, explaining what makes it so peaceful.

What is an important possession you have lost? Write an essay about that possession, explaining its importance to you.

What is one of your favorite possessions? Write an essay about that possession, explaining what makes it one of your favorites.

Explain the meaning of *bravery*.

Explain the importance of failure.

Explain the significance of responsibility.

Explain the effects of stress.

Explain the kinds of friendship.

Explain the value of hope.

Explain the sources of pride.

Explain the difficulties of trustworthiness.

Figure 7–2 Bank of Expository Prompts

What to Do Next

- Ask students to color-code their essays to show where they embedded different kinds of details, especially from your rubric: infoshots, or snapshots, or any of the text icons that you've worked on together in class (see pages 143–144 for text icons). In the example that follows, Juliette Miller's piece about her room contains embedded ba-da-bing sentences in her descriptions.

- Color-code together a high-scoring essay (download it from your state assessment website) to analyze informally the kinds of structures and details your state considers effective.

Student Samples

This is Juliette's detailed piece, based on her kernel essay. She detailed her kernel essay, using the ba-da-bing technique for each of her main body paragraphs.

Name __Juliette__

Expository Essay: Place

Think of one of your favorite places.
Write an essay explaining what makes this place so special.

Name your place: __My room__

Put your **text** structure here. Conversation: Comparing notes

Some people think...	And other people think...	But I think...	What I wonder is...	✕	✕

Write your **kernel essay** here.
1. Some people think my room is ugly.
2. Other people think my room is pretty.
3. I think my room is different but comfortable.
4. What I realize is what makes me love my room.
5.
6.

Plan for **details**:

Details to add to kernel essay		Infoshots	
☑ snapshots	☐ sensory details	☐ description	☐ synonyms/antonyms
☐ similes	☐ vocabulary words	☐ compare/contrast	☐ part/whole
	☐ combined	☐ cause/effect	☐ item/category
☐ ba-da-bings	·sentences	☐ before/after	☐ _____

Three signatures:
1. Juliette
2. Tamara
3. Sandra

Figure 7–3 Juliette's planning sheet

My Room

When I walk into my house, I go to my room and don't think about anything. But when people come over, I always wonder what their reaction will be.

The first time my friends say to me, "Is this your room?" with the reply of yes, they respond, "Oh," with a disgusted look on their face. As soon as I walk through the door, I take a look inside my room: to the left there's a Western saddle propped up on an antique trunk; a cowbell next to it on the trunk; a roping rope coiled up and looped over the horn of the saddle; on the wall, a collection of miniature cowboy items. I understand why people might think this isn't my room.

Or my friends will say, "Please tell me this is your room!" as I slightly nod with questions marks floating around in my head. They look at me and smile. As I walk through my room, I notice the collection of hot diggety dogs sitting on the window sill; a nice collection of jewelry on my vanity/dresser; purses of all designs and shapes hanging on hooks close to my bed; the little mini-flat screen across from my bed screaming "Juliette" on it. I can see why people like my room.

But then, I realize why should I care if my friends like my room or not. After all, I'm the one in it. The warmth of the carpet running through my toes, I walk to my bed and fall back onto it, my head hitting my panda bear pillow pet. I look at the ceiling and play my own movie there. I feel so hypnotized about the comfort of my room. Yeah, my room may be different, but it sure is comfortable.

Still, I wonder what it is that attracts people to like or dislike my room. Is it the horse-related stuff hanging on my walls? or the two beds that feel like floating high-in-the-sky clouds in my room for sleepovers?

I have come to the conclusion that no matter what your room looks like, everyone will have their opinions, and you will have yours. But out of everyone present, the one living in the room is most important.

—Juliette Miller, grade 7

Here are Juliette's ba-da-bing sentences, which she added.

As soon as I walk through the door, I take a look inside my room: to the left there's a Western saddle propped up on an antique trunk; a cowbell next to it on the trunk; a roping rope coiled up and looped over the horn of the saddle; on the wall, a collection of miniature cowboy items. I understand why people might think this isn't my room.

As I walk through my room, I notice the collection of hot diggety dogs sitting on the window sill; a nice collection of jewelry on my vanity/dresser; purses of all designs and shapes hanging on hooks close to my bed; the little mini-flat screen across from my bed screaming "Juliette" on it. Now I can see why people like my room.

The warmth of the carpet running through my toes, I walk to my bed and fall back onto it, my head hitting my panda bear pillow pet. I look at the ceiling and play my own movie there. I feel so hypnotized about the comfort of my room. Yeah, my room may be different, but it sure is comfortable.

Figure 7–4 Tamar's planning sheet

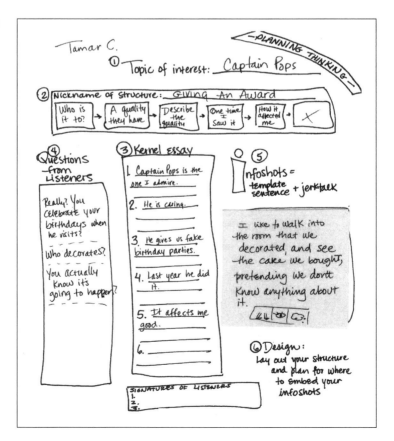

Captain Pops

This is an essay about someone I look up to most. My grandpa, Captain Pops. He's remarkably funny and sweet, and has the best ideas.

Captain Pop is caring, he always was. He doesn't surprise us, but he pretends to. He's very tall, with scraggly hair and has a really great smile.

Captain Pops gives us fake surprise birthday parties once a year, because he's not there for all of our real ones. We go to Toys R Us, get something, wrap it and hide it somewhere. Then when it starts its great. I like to walk into the room that we decorated, and see the cake we bought, pretend we didn't even know about this. It so cheerful and colorful, not to mention noisy.

I still love to see Captain Pop's smile and know he has a heart of gold. And that is why I admire him the most.

This quality affects me in a good way. I always love to laugh like a hyena around him telling jokes and doing magic tricks. But he has lots more qualities. He's retired, but I crave to be around my optimistic grandpa.

—Tamar C., grade 5

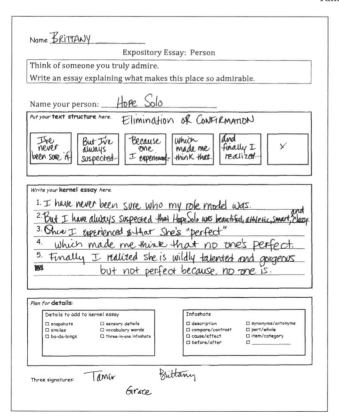

Figure 7–5 Brittany's planning sheet

Hope Solo

As a child I never quite knew what I wanted. One day it would be the new Disney Barbie princess doll Cinderella and the next a life size Cheer Care Bear. I went through stages questioning what I wanted to be a princess, a singer, a famous actress, an artist, and a photographer. Now as I am older I am influenced greatly by everything in the world. There are people who go with things and have no ambition, and people who work hard for what they want and succeed. Those are people who we all look up to, Role Models.

A role model is someone who has worked hard and achieved their dreams, and made a difference or an impression on the world. People who teach others how to be healthy, happy, and enjoy their lives and tell them that nothing is impossible if you work hard enough for what you want, it is no dream. My role model is Hope Solo, America's woman soccer team goal keeper. Not only is she a soccer player, she also appeared on Dancing with the Stars proving that soccer players are not just rough on the field but graceful on their feet. She is beautiful, athletic, smart, classy, and the most down to earth person. She gives inspirational advice to teens all over, and challenges everyone to get a good education to pursue their dreams.

Once I walked into my friend's room. As I glanced around her room eyeing all the Taylor Swift posters tapped on the walls I couldn't help noticing that the walls had staple holes punctured into it and the smell of fresh new paint overwhelmed her room. As we congregated to her couch we started talking. I was saying how Hope Solo was my role model. She looked at me and said "Well she's not perfect like Taylor Swift." Shocked by her unseemly response I thought "What is perfect?" To me it is an unrealistic word; nothing can ever be "Perfect."

Finally I realized that Hope Solo is one of the greatest role models for all children, adults, and teens. She is not cliché in any way possible, she is not perfect but she is unique and that's what makes her my role model.

Text Structures for Expository Essays Describing a Person

You may use one of these or any other structure on the Text Structures wall. Or create your own new one!

Some of my kids just have to know what kind of score they'll get, so I use this as a rubric. You can convert the points to whatever grade or scale works for you.

Prized Possession

I just couldn't do without . . .	It has the most . . .	It has . . .	Before I had it . . .	That's why . . .	Without it, I would . . .

Giving an Award

Who you choose	One quality they have	One moment when you saw that quality	How that moment affected you then	What you think of that person still

Evolution of a Term (word or phrase in the prompt)

What the word meant to me when I was four	When I was a little older	What the word means to me now	What the word will probably mean when I am _____ (pick an age)

Explanation of a Term

Dictionary-like definition	Your personal definition	What feeling you get from it	What others make you think	Example in society today	Another example (optional)

Cary Inzerello

What is it? (Defining a Word)

Is it this?	Or this?	Or this?	A memory	Which makes me realize it's this

Adrian Martinez

Figure 7–6 Text structures for expository essays

Name: _____

Checking Your Essay

ORGANIZATION AND STRUCTURE	One paragraph for each kernel sentence?	Is your planning sheet attached? (text structure boxes and kernel essay)	**8 points**	
DEPTH	2 or more 3-in-1 infoshots?	Highlight yellow	**8 points**	
	2 snapshots?	Highlight blue	**4 points**	
WORD CHOICE	3 or more vocabulary words?	Underline these	**4 points**	
MECHANICS	Periods? Proper nouns capitalized? Apostrophes correct?		**4 points**	
PROOFREADING	3 "I heard this" signatures?	Did you listen as you read?	**2 points**	
FORMAT	Is your heading on the top left?	Title centered, capitalized, and not underlined?		

Total: 30 points

Figure 7–7 "Checking your essay" rubric

Name _Silver_

week of.
11/9
Silver - L.A.

Planning Sheet: Food Award Essay

Put your **truism** *here*

Jim's has the best pancakes in
town,

Put your **text structure** *here:* Sensory Conclusions

| What I see | What I smell | What I taste | How does it Feel | What I thought | What I recommend |

Silver, Rosenberg
and Wendy

Write your **kernel essay** *here.*

1. I see warm, steamy, fluffy pancakes in the oven.
2. There is a sweet aroma coming from my plate.
3. In my mouth a creamy pancake to my delight.
4. It tastes like a creamy taste is soaring through my mouth.
5. I thought I had a splendid meal.
6. My recommendation is to try it once, and see if anyone likes it.

Plan for **details**:

Action Detail

☐ snapshots   ☐ sensory details
☐ thoughtshots   ☐ ba-da-bing
☐ dialogue   ☐ _____

Infoshots

☐ description   ☐ synonyms/antonyms
☐ compare/contrast ☐ part/whole
☐ cause/effect   ☐ item/category
☐ before/after   ☐ _____

Silver   _alex_   _maggie_

Figure 7–8 Silver's planning sheet

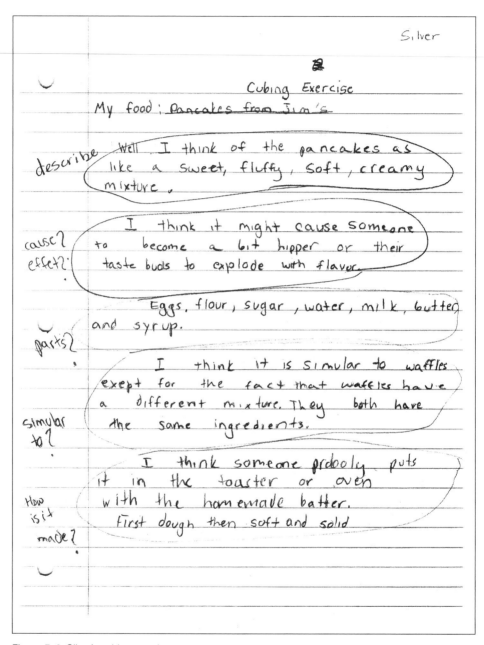

Silver

Cubing Exercise

My food: Pancakes from Jim's

describe — Well I think of the pancakes as like a sweet, fluffy, soft, creamy mixture.

cause?
effet? — I think it might cause someone to become a bit hipper or their taste buds to explode with flavor.

parts? — Eggs, flour, sugar, water, milk, butter and syrup.

simular to? — I think it is simular to waffles exept for the fact that waffles have a different mixture. They both have the same ingredients.

How is it made? — I think someone probuly puts it in the toaster or oven with the homemade batter. First dough then soft and solid

Figure 7-9 Silver's cubing exercise

Silver

11-9

Ms. Bernabei

Language Arts-5

Pancake Wonders

I see warm, steamy, fluffy pancakes in the oven. There is a waitress in a white skirt, red smock, and a pin that says Betty, blond hair, and a hat with a smile on her face. While coloring I looked at my mother and she said that's so beautiful. All of a sudden I turned and saw piping hot pancakes right next to me.

There is a sweet <u>aroma</u> coming from my plate. The fresh scent is swirling in the air. I smell the maple syrup as it is pouring onto my melting butter. Butter surrounds my fruit causing a <u>tropical</u> smell.

In my mouth there finally is a creamy pancake to my delight. Biting into a warm blueberry caused it to burst. The blueberry syrup, butter, and pancake unite and there is a <u>celebration</u> of flavors. 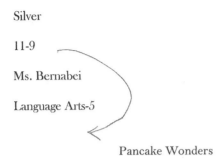 Blueberry, strawberry, chocolate, creamy, fluffy, and steamy pancakes and waffles are the same, but flatter and filled with love.

I am glad I chose the soft pancakes because I have several loose teeth. The last time I ate a crispy waffle my tooth fell out and it left a <u>crevice</u>. Pancakes are almost the same as waffles.

While enjoying my splendid <u>beverage</u> of steaming hot chocolate and the final bite of my blueberry pancake I begin to plan my next visit to Jim's. I will be returning to Jim's on Wednesday evening when kids eat for free.

I recommend Jim's because the blueberry pancakes remind me of summer.

Figure 7–10 Silver's first draft

Pancake Wonders

I see warm, steamy, fluffy pancakes in the oven. There is a waitress in a white shirt, red smock, and a pin that says Betty, blond hair, and a hat with a smile on her face. While coloring I looked at my mother and she said that's so beautiful. All of a sudden I turned and saw piping hot pancakes right next to me.

There is a sweet aroma coming from my plate. The fresh scent is swirling in the air. I smell the maple syrup as it is pouring onto my melting butter. Butter surrounds my fruit causing a tropical smell.

In my mouth there finally is a creamy pancake to my delight. Biting into a warm blueberry caused it to burst. The blueberry syrup, butter, and pancake unite and there is a celebration of flavors.

I am glad I chose the soft pancakes because I have several loose teeth. The last time I ate crispy waffle my tooth fell out and it left a crevice.

While enjoying my splendid beverage of steaming hot chocolate and a final bite of my blueberry pancake I begin to plan my next visit to Jim's. I will be returning to Jim's on Wednesday evening when kids eat for free.

I recommend Jim's because the blueberry pancakes remind me of summer.

—Silver Rosenberg, grade 5

What is your favorite game? My favorite game is Zombie in the Woods. I know you're probably thinking what in the world is that. It's my favorite because it's outside, fun, and the chills. Now hide quick or the zombies will get you while I explain why it's my favorite game and what it is.

To begin with it's an outside game. You hide in the woods while the person counts, but you can have them spin in circles with their eyes close too. Any way it's a very energetic game because you don't want to get infected. It's like hide and seek tag. Just there is no base and you pretend to bite the person. One time when I was playing with my friends. Somebody fast was it so I sprinted like a deer. Feeling scared and stupid because it was only a game. I was fast and didn't get caught, but others weren't as lucky.

In addition it's fun. It's fun because it's new and different. The game is made of just other games. It's new because I just created it. When my friends and me were bored of the same game we decided to make up a new one. After a while of thinking of a bunch of different games. I combined them to get the ultimate game Zombie in the Woods. For example we were bored of tag one day and played that and it was awesome. I couldn't believe how much fun we had. We almost played for 2 hours straight.

Equally important it gives you chills. I know it's probably stupid to get chills from a game, but you have obviously never played it. Your heart pumps one million miles per hour. Waiting quietly and nervously for the zombie to attack it's next victim. While you wait you feel that they will pop out of nowhere at you. It's like manhunt, but maybe even creepier. Just when you think your safe the zombie comes out of the blue for you. I remember when I played it with my friends I was frantic that I could pee my pants, but then the zombie could get me. Also it is not solving my problems. It felt like a life or death game and I darted away like crazy because I was absorbed in the game over my head. When I play I stay alert and keep up my guard.

As you can see Zombie in the Woods is my favorite game because it's outside, it's fun, and it gives you chills. I hope you want to play it now, but watch out you don't know who is the next victim. The zombie could be lurking in the shadows ready to strike right now. Maybe your next.

—*Bonnie Walden, grade 4*

8 Open Essay

If You Want Them to Make All of the Choices

Basic Steps

1. Students write truism/thesis
2. Choose structure from all choices
3. Kernel essay (write/share)
4. Flesh out with details

Tools

- "Build-a-Prompt" sheet
- Opinion text structures
- Kernel essay planning sheet
- "Planning Thinking" sheet

Setting the Scene

You would like your students to do it all: come up with their own prompt, choose their own structure, design their own plan for details, the works. And you'd like for the results to be clear and powerful. Maybe your students already know how to write a kernel essay from a text structure or maybe they need a little guidance.

Step One: Gathering Truisms, or the Plain Paper Bag of Truths

The Point

To start with the right hand, or "what we know," teachers often offer students prompts in the form of wise sayings or life lessons to be used as discussion topics. But students can generate these themselves. This exercise will provide a classroom with a bank of student-written truisms, useful throughout the year.

Teaching It

- "Today we're going to explore some things we think are true. Take out a sheet of paper and number it from 1 to 10." *(Write* family *and* friends *on the board.)*

- "Tell me, what else in your lives is important to you? On your paper, see if you can list ten things that are important to you, in addition to family and friends. Give it a try. You have three minutes." *(Wait.)*

- "How many did you think of?" *(Share.)*

- "Now we're going to look at these and turn them into sentences by asking one question: What is one surprising thing you've learned about it? Let's do the first two together."

Figure 8-1 Two hands illustration

- *(Model, by pointing to the word* family *on the board.)* "Hmm, what is one surprising thing I've learned about family? All families are not alike. I did learn that. I used to think that all kids had parents like mine, but when I went to college, I saw that it wasn't true at all. I remember being surprised about how rare it was to have kindhearted parents. So that's one surprising thing I learned about family." *(Write down "Kindhearted parents are rare.")* "There. There's one."

- "Friends? Hmm . . . what surprising thing have I learned about friends?" *(If students blurt out truths, use them. Otherwise make one up like, "Sometimes friends are still friends even if they disappoint you." Write it on the board.)*

- "Now look at your list. Do the same thing. Ask yourself, 'What's one surprising thing I've learned about this?' See how many sentences you can write."

(Share, collect, and type up the sentences. Cut them apart, and fill a paper bag with them.)

Debriefing

- "Was it easy to think of truths about your words?"
- "Were any difficult?"
- "Looking at your sentences, do you consider some more interesting than others?"
- "What makes them more interesting?"

Student Samples

Truisms from Charlie Boggess' first-period English I class, ninth graders:

- You can't do everything by yourself, and you need to trust your teammates.
- Even though we live in different countries, that will never end our friendship.
- Sometimes things happen for a reason.
- If you are patient, good things will come.
- Being there for special moments can make you proud to be in your family.
- Sometimes you need to take responsibility for your actions and accept the consequences.
- Things that seem to happen for the worse can be really for the better.
- People can make you feel special and important to them without meaning to.
- A child's first word can be an unforgettable memory.
- Life does not stop for one person; it will take and give things to you. It's your choice to accept the challenge it gives you.
- Things don't always go the way you want them to, but it would be nice if they did.
- Sometimes when people do something embarrassing, it can be hilarious.
- Putting your foot down can be the best thing to do.
- Sometimes floaties aren't the best for the beach.
- Sometimes throwing sand isn't such a good idea.
- Sometimes you can't really go too fast on skis.
- People can make really funny faces.

Spin-offs

- Before cutting up the sentences, students can share, shop for truths they like, and copy them into their journals.
- If you are reading literature, students can create sentences that the characters might consider surprising truths about the world.

- As a pleasant alternative, you can distribute quotation books and allow students time to enjoy reading these. As they find quotations they'd like to share with each other, they copy those into their journals for sharing. When they accumulate five or more, they have ready banks of quotations for use as the truism in this exercise.

Step Two: **Developing a Kernel Essay**

The Point

Once students have selected a truism, they are ready to figure out how they know it's true. Giving them a limited choice of structures allows them a "safe" way to develop the new skill, writing kernel essays. If they are already skilled at how to do this, you can give them more choices, even unlimited choices.

Figure 8–2
Planning sheet

The Story of My Thinking

| What I used to think | But this happened | So now I think |

Figure 8–3
The Story of My Thinking text structure

Conversation: Comparing Notes

| Some people think . . . | Other people think . . . | I think . . . | What I wonder is . . . |

Figure 8–4
Comparing Notes text structure

Evolution of a Term (word or phrase in the prompt)

| What the word meant to me when I was four | What it meant when I was a little older | What the word means to me now | What the word will probably mean when I am ___ (pick an age) |

Figure 8–5
Evolution of a Term text structure

Teaching It

(Distribute planning sheets; students can also use regular lined paper.)

- "Write your truism or quotation at the top of the planning sheet."
- "The next step is to select a text structure that will work for you. How do you know what will work? I'll show you."
- "Let's look at Joe's. He elected to use a quotation as his truism. So it's your turn to choose one of these three structures. Here are your choices." *(Show them the three structures at the top.)*
- "Then you'll write one sentence per box, as Joe did."
- *(After writing.)* "Now it's time to collect listener signatures. Write 'I heard this' near the bottom of your page. Let three different people hear your kernel essay. Have them sign near the 'I heard this.' These can be members of your family, classmates, friends, anyone. If you don't have time to collect all of your signatures during class, it's your homework."

Figure 8–6 Joe's planning sheet, "Adults"

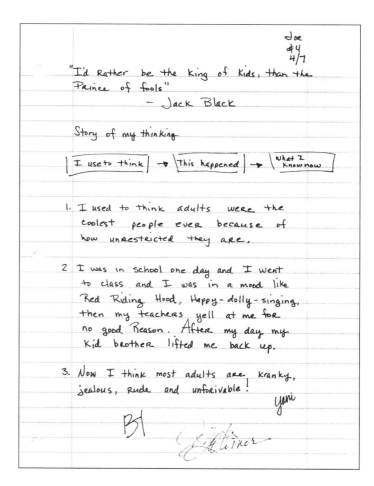

Debriefing

- "Is it surprising to you that you could accomplish so much in just a few sentences?"

Student Samples

(See Joe's.)

Spin-off

Let students use the build-a-prompt page to create alternative prompts leading to their own opinion truisms, either as themselves or as characters from literature.

This is a display of the four steps involved in writing a kernel essay responding to a quotation.

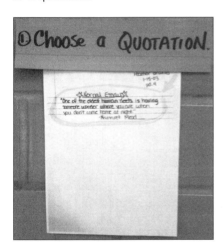
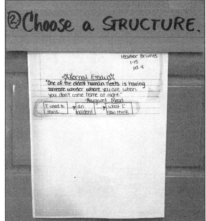
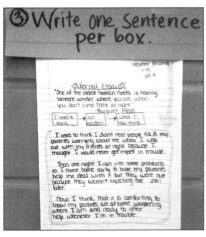
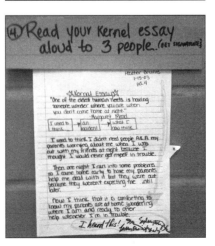

Figure 8–7 Steps in writing kernel essay (four steps in four photographs)

Name __Joseph, grade 7__

Planning Sheet

Type of Writing (Check One)

☐ Writing about myself   ☐ Writing to inform me   ☑ Writing to inform others   ☐ Writing to persuade   ☐ Writing about literature

Put your **truism** *(aka assertion aka problem aka main question)* here

~~I~~ Sometimes first impressions are right.

Put your **text structure** here.   Burst of Recognition

| What you saw | What you thought | What you recognized | What you wanted to do | — | — |

by Joseph Klein

Write your **kernel essay** here.

1. I saw really comfy chairs.
2. I thought it will be cool.
3. I recognized no negative things.
4. I actually wanted to work.
5.
6.

Plan for **details**:

Action Detail

☐ snapshots   ☐ sensory details
☐ thoughtshots   ☐ ba-da-bing
☐ dialogue   ☐ _____

Infoshots

☐ description   ☐ synonyms/antonyms
☐ compare/contrast   ☐ part/whole
☐ cause/effect   ☐ item/category
☐ before/after   ☐ _____

Figure 8–8 Joe's planning sheet, "Classroom"

Joe decided to write about a classroom he liked (mine!), but after shopping for a structure, he decided that none of the available structures did what he needed them to. He came in the next day wondering if he would be in trouble because he invented his own text structure. We celebrated another first in our room, and students have been creating their own structures ever since.

Classroom

On the first day of school I was scared because I had a lot of new teachers and my mom kept telling me that I have a language arts teacher that knows everything you can imagine related to language arts. I let that pass right through my head. When I walked in to school on the first day, my friends and I were walking down the hallway and we saw the coolest room ever. It was unlike the other rooms. It was organized. I was shocked. The teacher had relaxing chairs and unlike other teachers trusted us. When it was time for that teacher's class I got so happy. That teacher was awesome she gave us work that she knew we would be capable of doing but it is not too hard and not too easy. In the beginning of the year I thought I would have to cope with learning in her class. After a week I figured out learning is fun when you get the right teacher so then I started thinking to myself, "Will she do what my mom has been trying to get teachers to get me to do my whole life in one week?"

After a week or two passed, my best friend told me, "Come on! Look at Mrs. Bernabei's room. Run!" I was wondering what was wrong but then I saw rainbows then I thought in my head that this has proved once again that Mrs. Bernabei's room is one of my favorite places on earth.

—*Joseph Klein, grade 7*

Chocolate, Chocolate, Chocolate

As I bite into a Hershey's kiss, I can't help but think, "There must be more to this." I am not just biting into a teardrop shaped piece of milk chocolate. I am biting into the future of civilization. Chocolate is a game changer. Chocolate can make the world's problems dissolve.

Most products, including almost every type of food, have a social impact on the world. Chocolate's social impact just happens to be good. Many wealthy countries, like China and not the USA, isolate poorer countries instead of helping them. Switzerland is cool though, so they lend them a helping hand. The countries of Cote d'Ivoire and Ghana produce 59% of the world's cocoa. In Cote d'Ivoire and in Ghana, the majority of the population lives below the poverty line. This could be changed if China and another country like Switzerland bought a whole bunch of chocolate. The government would be so happy that countries are finally paying attention to them, they would become uncorrupt and dole out their new cocoa money to the starving inhabitants of their countries.

On a smaller scale, do you know those days when everything seems horrible? Like you walk into class, and you see that you have a test that you forgot about. You rake your brain for the answers, but you can't remember: you didn't study. Well, come over to me and I probably have a hunk of chocolate on my person. Eat the chocolate. Chocolate intake has been linked with release of serotonin in the brain, which is thought to produce feelings of pleasures. Intellectually, you reason with yourself that the test doesn't matter that much and you'll study next time. The chestnut brown milk chocolate just beats the test in any race known to man. Dang, is chocolate good or what?

Chocolate is so good in fact, that people harbor addictions to it. But don't do that. Chocolate is good, but not good enough that you need to join an anonymous group and talk about how much you love it. Just savor the chocolate and relax. Chocolate is good and now, just by reading this amazing essay that originated from a cocoa bean essay (kernel essay), you might not even need the chocolate. Just kidding, eat the chocolate.

—*Eileen Stolow, grade 8*

Build-an-Opinion Prompt Examples for To Kill a Mockingbird, *written by ninth graders:*

Why I dislike apologizing—by Scout Finch

Why I enjoy gossiping—by Aunt Alexandra

Why I love summertime—by Scout Finch

Why I crave freedom—by Tom Robinson

Why I enjoy party time—by Jem Finch

Why I crave cats—by Arthur "Boo" Radley

Why I enjoy pondering—by Atticus Finch

Why I need a new house—by Ms. Maudie

Why I enjoy watching over the Finch children—by Arthur "Boo" Radley

Why I think mysteries are important—by Jem Finch

Why I abhor sunrise—by Boo Radley

Why I like my backyard—by Scout Finch

Why I did Tom Robinson case—by Atticus Finch

Why I crave for my birthday to come—by Dill

Why I enjoy reading—by Scout Finch

Why I enjoy responsibility—by Calpurnia

Why I enjoy freedom—by Jem Finch

Why I enjoy friendship—by Scout Finch

Why I like tree houses—by Jem Finch

Why I dislike playing with Scout—by Jem Finch

Why I enjoy spying—by Scout Finch

Why I dislike school—by Scout Finch

Why I like respect—by Atticus Finch

Why I like talking to Miss Maudie—by Scout Finch

Why I honor/respect my father—by Atticus Finch

Why I would like to live on an island—by Atticus Finch

Why I enjoy electronics—by Jem Finch

Why I detest awards—by Atticus Finch

Why I dislike school—by Scout Finch

Why I crave acceptance—by Arthur Radley

Why I need to know how to shoot a gun—by Atticus Finch

Why I crave to understand the color of my skin—by Tom Robinson

Why I enjoy chocolate—by Atticus Finch

Why I need the summer—by Dill

Why I hate court—by Tom Robinson

Why I don't need boxing lessons—by Scout Finch

Why I despise school—by Scout Finch

Why I like food—by Walter Cunningham

Why I dislike the 1930s—by Atticus Finch

Why I dislike dresses—by Scout Finch

Build an Opinion Prompt

Explain why I	(choose one)	(choose one)
	☐ crave	☐ times
	☐ need	☐ things—possessions
	☐ enjoy	☐ activities
	☐ like	☐ places
	☐ dislike	☐ abstract concepts
	☐ detest	
	☐ abhor	

TIMES	POSSESSIONS	ACTIVITIES	PLACES	ABSTRACT CONCEPTS
1898 (or another year)	awards	apologizing	airport	acceptance
afternoon	basketball	biking	backyard	bravery
birthdays	cameras	cooking	beach	caring
breakfast	candy	crying	beauty shop	confusion
early morning	chocolate	dreaming	bookstore	disappointment
far into the future	electronics	exercising	car	embarrassment
last semester	food	falling	college	envy
last week	furniture	gossiping	country	excitement
last year	glasses	hopping	dollhouse	failure
naptime	gym bag	interrupting	ecosystems	fear
nighttime	jewelry	jumping	front seat	freedom
noon	junk	laughing	gardens	friendship
now	library books	painting	gas station	frustration
party time	money	planning	grocery store	happiness
study time	movies	pondering	highway	honor
summertime	pets	reading	islands	hope
sunrise	plants	running	Jacuzzi	independence
sunset	rugs	sewing	land	loneliness
today	school supplies	shopping	library	love
tomorrow	shoes	singing	mine shaft	loyalty
Tuesday	skates	skating	mountains	patriotism
when i was younger	towel	sleeping	movie theatre	pride
winter	toys	smiling	north	respect
years ago	trash can	spying	ocean	responsibility
yesterday		swimming	park	stress
		talking	place of worship	trustworthiness
		texting	pool	worry
		thinking	rain forest	
		washing hands	rooms	
		watching movies/TV	seashore	
		whispering	sports arena	
		wishing	tree house	
		writing	underwater	

Figure 8–9 *Build-an-opinion prompt chart*

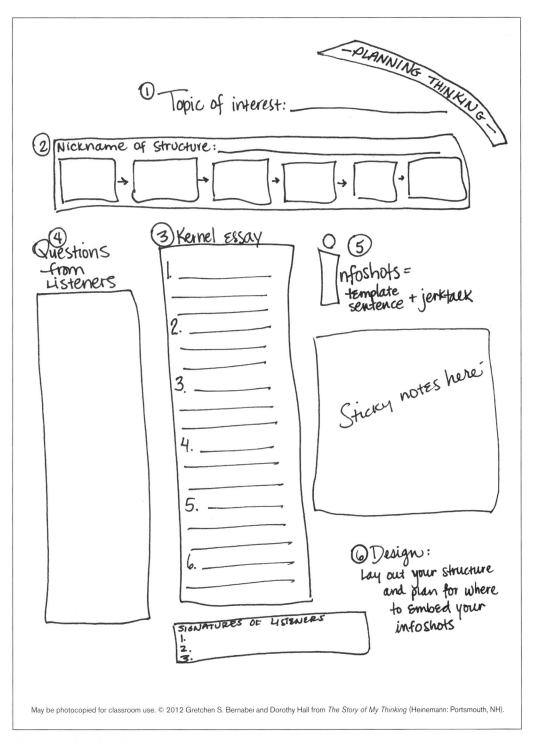

Figure 8–10 Planning thinking sheet

9 Cubing

If You Want Them to Focus on Developing a Body of Informational Content

1. Cubing infoshots
2. Follow-up assignment for polish
3. Retrace steps by keeping/putting infoshot templates into writer's notebooks or journals

Tool

- ""Analogy Patterns for Infoshots" sheet

Setting the Scene

You're painfully aware that good expository writing is dense with information, but your students are having difficulty getting beyond "I really like it because it's so nice, which makes me like it." You want to build their descriptive and analytical muscles, to help them think about any given topic from multiple angles, so that they'll know what to do when it's time for details.

The Point

When it's time to add informative details about objects, students may not know what to do. Sometimes inexperienced writers will simply add adjectives because they don't know what other kinds of information to include. This exercise will familiarize them with the patterns of information, giving them a format that every student can use. This exercise is an adaptation of "cubing," first published by Elizabeth Cowan in *Writing* (1980).

Teaching It

(For this activity, each student will need to focus on one object. It can be the same object for the whole class, or you can distribute different small objects to everyone.)

Figure 9–1 Analogy patterns for infoshots

- "Look at the object. I'm going to ask you to write about it, for three minutes at a time. First, describe it. What does it look like? You have three minutes." *(Time them and stop at the end of three minutes.)*

- "Next, skip a line. What is it used for? Write as many different uses as you can think of for this object in the next three minutes." *(Time them and stop at the end of three minutes.)*

- "Next, skip a line. What are its parts? Think of as many different ways as you can to separate out parts of this object. You have three minutes." *(Time them and stop at the end of three minutes.)*

- "Next, skip a line. What is it similar to? Think of as many different things as you can that this object resembles. What is it like? You have three minutes." *(Time them and stop at the end of three minutes.)*

- "Next, skip a line. What can it cause? Think of as many different things as you can that this item might possibly cause. You have three minutes." *(Time them and stop at the end of three minutes.)*

- "Next, skip a line. This is the last part. How has this item changed in any way? How has it transformed? Look at it and think to yourself, 'before and after.' What did it used to be in the past? What could it change into in the future? You have three minutes." *(Time them and stop at the end of three minutes.)*

- "What you did just now was a version of an exercise called 'cubing.' We used some of the most common relationships for these six steps. There are other relationships, but I selected these six today."

(Share either in partners or groups, and then share a few with the whole group.)

Debriefing

- "Are you surprised at how much you found to say about this object?"
- "Could these questions help you if you needed to talk about something?"

What to Do Next

- Revise the papers into "all about" articles, using the "Titles That Sell" sheet from the appendix to help set the tone.
- Do sentence-combining exercises with some of the stubbier sentences.

- An idea from Jody Giles, extraordinary English teacher at Alamo Heights High School: have the students include participial phrases and vocabulary words in the revised pieces.

Spin-offs

Ask two students to circle their two favorite chunks of text to use as two body paragraphs in a short essay about the object. All they'll need to add is an introduction, a conclusion, and minor transitions.

For variety, assign groups one infoshot pattern sentence, and have the whole class write sentences about the same object. (See the dogtag example, on pages 92–93.) Collect the sentences and have students draw from the sentences (combining them, improving them) to produce essays about the object. As a class, survey the results and see what you notice.

Figure 9–2
Analogy patterns

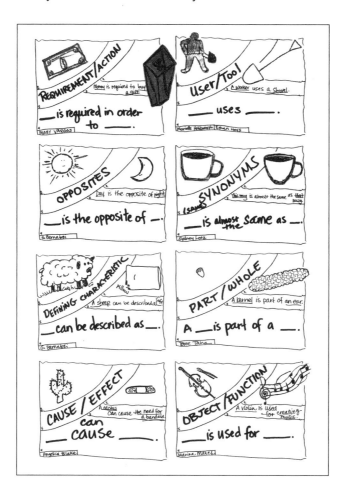

Student Samples

These next three examples were written by fourth graders.

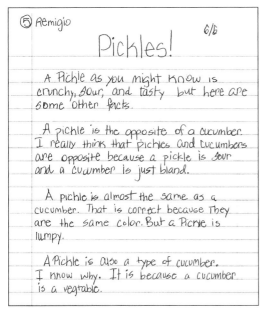

⑤ Remigio   6/6

Pickles!

A Pichle as you might know is crunchy, sour, and tasty but here are some other facts.

A pichle is the opposite of a cucumber. I really think that pichles and cucumbers are opposite because a pickle is sour and a cuwmber is just bland.

A pichle is almost the same as a cucumber. That is correct because They are the same color. But a Picnie is lumpy.

A Pichle is also a type of cucumber. I hnow why. It is because a cucumber is a vegtable.

Figure 9–3 Pickles

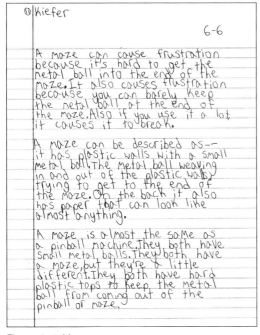

⑪ Kiefer   6-6

A maze can cause frustration because it's hard to get the metal ball into the end of the maze. It also couses flustration because you can barely keep the metal ball at the end of the maze. Also if you use it a lot, it causes it to break.

A maze can be described as--it has plastic walls with a small metal ball. The metal ball weaving in and out of the plastic walls, trying to get to the end of the maze. On the back it also has paper that can look like almost anything.

A maze is almost the same as a pinball nachine. They both have small metal balls. They both have a maze, but they're a little different. They both have hard plastic tops to keep the metal ball from coming out of the pinball or maze.

Figure 9–4 Mazes

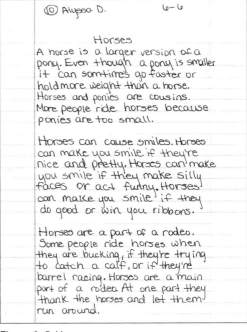

⑩ Alyssa D.   6-6

Horses

A horse is a larger version of a pony. Even though a pony is smaller it can somtimes go faster or holdmore weight than a horse. Horses and ponies are cousins. More people ride horses because ponies are too small.

Horses can cause smiles. Horses can make you smile if they're nice and pretty. Horses can make you smile if they make silly faces or act funny. Horses can make you smile if they do good or win you ribbons.

Horses are a part of a rodeo. Some people ride horses when they are bucking, if they're trying to catch a calf, or if they're barrel racing. Horses are a main part of a rodeo. At one part they thank the horses and let them run around.

Figure 9–5 Horses

The next pieces were written by twelfth graders, whose teacher asked them to revise their cubing pieces for clarity and beauty and to include participial phrases and vocabulary words.

Carlos's Owl

Creature of the night, augmented in darkness, the owl is a mysterious creature. The guardian of night sees all with his 360 degree view, not missing a thing. The furtive owl hovers in the night sky, waiting, stalking, savoring his meal to come. With his sharp claws and keen eyesight, it spots and pierces the skin of his prey.

With a hoot cold as ice, striking fear in his enemies and serenity to his friends. The owl delivers the message to his commander. The owl, a stealthy beast, travels vast distances to win battles. The owl flapped his wings for hours, relentless, determined, a perfect sign of wisdom.

Hooting, he warns the night crawlers of his presence. The owl, lets the forest know no one is safe under the cover of the night sky, takes his time to choose his victim. He flies above them all, hungry.

The owl's presence causes children to tremble. Small creatures to search for sanctuary, to cower behind something darker than night. Causes disturbance in a peaceful campers sleep. Make them be alert.

The life of an owl starts in a dark oval shell. Warrior at birth he fights his way through the same barrier than once kept him safe, but now stop him from seeing sunlight and keeps him from filling his lungs with air. Now, sits on a nest helplessly. Taking a leap of faith, he jumps off a tree, spreads his small wings, flapping his wings furiously try to grasp air and then starts to fly.

—*Carlos Puentes, grade 12*

The Truth About a Sippy Cup

The sippy cup is mostly white, covered with bright red cherries and hearts. It is topped with a bright red top, so that the cup won't spill its contents, on which bite marks have inhabited the spout. The handle, a darkened piece of plastic, is disproportional to the actual cup. When the top of the sippy cup is opened there is nothing in it to be spilled.

The sippy cup could be used for children so they can prevent a spill, although I have seen a group of elderly who drink from sippy cups to make them feel younger. The truth is that the sippy cup is used for parents so they deal with less mess from their children.

Appreciated by mothers, the sippy cup is a part of childhood around the toddler age when children are too old for bottles. It describes children in how kids are messy yet innocent, because it's there nature. From Disney to Marvel, these plastic dishes have become very popular, a part of a whole kitchen set.

An ingenious invention, the sippy cup can cause a prevention of a mess on the carpet in the living room. It could cause a child to be sad or happy depending on its contents. A copious amount of sippy cups can be found under the seat of a car, exploding from heat, causing it to jettison out the window.

The sippy cup came from an adult, a parent who, dreamt of a world where children were not messy, and did her best to make that happen. A balding woman, mother of six, invented the "sippy cup" which became a huge success.

—*Reuben Uribes, grade 12*

The Truth About Rings

A ring symbolizes many different things and has much meaning to it. This little object has two main colors, silver or gold. Some have another color added, depending on the meaning and what it symbolizes.

People have different reasons for wearing rings: being married, showing religion or supporting a championship team. Some wear it just to catch people's attention, for example, a class ring.

Part of the jewelry category, rings can be used as gifts. Around the holidays you might see more jewelry than you see daily. Folks tend to show out or go all out, dress nicer, or just be seasonal. It's not just the holidays though, you'll really see them out and shining at special events like Sweet 16s, proms and graduations.

A necklace, used for the same purposes, is a more visible accessory. Let's not forget earrings, categorized with rings and necklaces. They are the most bought object in this category. Rings are similar and can relate to any other jewelry, simply because they are fashionable, religious and hold much meaning.

Jewelry, don't we love it? Folks extol jewelry, and sometimes they hold collections of them. Rings, grabbing our attention every day, get the best of us!

—*Eddie Moreno, grade 12*

If your group seems low in energy, you can turn this into a large-group exercise. The whole class will focus on one object, and the infoshots will be divided up and assigned one to a group. The group's goal is to create a number of sentences like the pattern sentence (e.g., ___ is a part of ___.). After just a few minutes, ask one representative from each group to bring their sentences to the front. Listen to each person's list. See the example, when a group of teachers focused on one set of dog tags, and wrote their lists. Personifying the steps like this makes the work playful, quick, and fruitful.

▶ LARGE-GROUP CUBING LESSON: DOG TAGS

Defining Characteristic
A dog tag can be described as medium built and Hispanic
A dog tag is about 5'11"
A dog tag has brown hair and brown eyes
A dog tag weighs 185 lbs.
A dog tag . . . the blood that runs through its veins is Type A
A dog tag . . . its heart's only purpose is to beat for you
A dog tag . . . hold on to me, never forget me
That dog tag is me

Extreme Degrees
Dog tags are a substitute version of a hero
Dog tags are a subtle version of tragedy
Dog tags are a literal version of a soldier's service
Dog tags are a perfect version of patriotism
Dog tags are a symbolic version of my father-in-law
Dog tags are a symbolic version of a brave person

Object/Use
Dog tags are used to identify a soldier in case he is separated from his squad
Dog tags help animals to find their way back to their owners

Transformation

Dog tags can change into jewelry—necklace, ring, bracelet, earrings, pin

Dog tags can change into a key chain

Dog tags can change into a memory

Dog tags can change into a memento

Dog tags can change into a decoration

Dog tags can change into a job label

Dog tags can change into an heirloom

Dog tags can change into a button

Dog tags can change into identification

Synonyms

Dog tags are a human version of "If lost, please return to sender"

Opposite

The opposite of dog tags are John Doe markers on graves

The opposite of dog tags is the Tomb of the Unknown Soldier

The opposite of dog tags is being left out

The opposite of dog tags is being unknown or lost

The opposite of dog tags is being disconnected from a group

The opposite of dog tags is being alone

The opposite of dog tags is circles

The opposite of dog tags is unidentified

The opposite of dog tags is loss of hope

This page helps students find titles to shape the tone of their pieces.

Titles That Sell Informational Articles

All About _____ and Why It Matters

Everything You Need to Know About _____

What You Never Knew About _____

Top Ten Reasons for _____

The Secret(s) Behind _____

The Truth About _____

Amazing Facts About _____

The Real Story About _____

The _____ Controversy

Your Personal Guide to _____

Success with _____

Win Big with _____

Prizewinning _____

The Ultimate Scoop on _____

Hidden Secrets About _____

An Essential Guide to _____

The Zen of _____

_____ for Dummies

Lessons from a _____

Just Say No to _____

Little Known Facts About _____

The Secret Life of _____

Figure 9-6 Titles That Sell

These infoshots provide choices to use in the cubing exercise.

Figure 9–7 Analogy Patterns

All the Horses History

Horses are a very large mammal that can be multiple different colors. Black and brown, tan and white there are so many different looks and types of horses in the world today. They have cores hair and long tails that seem to always be swiping at something.

Horses have been used for many different things over their lifespan. They first started off as a way of transportation for people. Before cars and planes and trains horses were really the only way to get around fast from place to place. Now day's people use them for entertainment just as much or more than transportation.

They can be part of many different things, such as a family pet or even the prizewinner in a rodeo. Some people just adore horses and want to take care of them a breed them so they are part of a breeding family. Family's will have copious amounts of different types and breeds or horses. Others use them as help on a ranch or a big farm.

Horses are very similar to other animals. They are kind of like ponies and mules; they all can do around the same things. Such as transporting people or objects to were they need to be.

Riding or having a horse can cause many different things. It obviously causes travel, to get from one place to another. It can cause entertainment for people, because some people just love to watch horses race or be ridden in some sort of event, but negligence can cause a bad injury if you mess around and get knocked off. It always can cause work being done if they horse is able to carry or haul something that a person is not able to

Throughout the lives of horses they have come very far in what they have done. From being just a source of travel to people they have developed in the mind of people as pets and as entertainment. They help families get jobs done and allow little children to fall in love with them.

—Laura Hurst, grade 4

The following papers were written by ninth graders after the cubing exercises. They chose their own topics and wrote papers, using the cubing technique on their own choices of infoshots pattern sentences. Then they revised and shaped their essays.

Tears for Dummies

In today's society it is okay for women to cry and shed tears. Yet the big manly men seem like the one thing they can't do is cry. I myself try to be one of those big tough guys that is without tear ducts. I actually haven't cried in years but I think there have been days where I could have shed a few tears, yet I've held myself together. Crying isn't a bad thing. Crying is a part of your emotions.

There are many reasons for us to cry. One is the obvious, because you are sad. The other is because of pain. I used to cry when I was little when I used to scrape myself from some falls. Now at the first sign of blood loss I just take it and not think about it.

Those are the negatives about crying, but there is also positives. Many people cry when they are extremely happy. Some examples are newlyweds, someone returning home from the Army, or just something special someone else has done for that person. When I go to church some people cry because of how uplifted they are. I'm sure there's more than that, but that is the most noticeable reason.

There is nothing wrong with a good weep when the occasion calls for it, but there is something wrong if you are just an emotionless body without feelings. Emotions and feelings are a part of being a human being. It would only be natural to be one with them and accept them.

—*Bruno Fontana, grade 9*

Everything You Need to Know About Honey

Honey is a dense, slow-moving liquid that is sweet and sugary. It's a light, translucent, golden color. Sometimes it comes in little bear-shaped bottles. I think bears are associated with honey because they like it. Honey is sticky if you get it on your clothes but it tastes great as a flavoring or spread on bread with butter.

Honey is naturally made in a beehive, but bee farmers buy honeybees and put them in a beehive simulator type thing, and then they harvest they honey. They have to wear suits and veils covering all the skin on their bodies so that the bees can't sting them.

When I eat something with honey on it or in it I can taste the distinctive taste. Honey is very sweet. Honey reminds me of the times at my dad's house in Blanco, Texas when my stepmom makes cornbread and drizzles honey over it.

Honey is a part of a bee's beehive. It's a part of a honey butter chicken biscuit from Whataburger, which are amazing by the way. The word honey is a part of a plant's name: the honeysuckle. The honeysuckle is called a honeysuckle because it tastes sweet like honey.

In years to come I think honey will become more popular as a sweetener. When you go to the honey section at a health foods store they have very many varieties of honey you've probably never heard of. Soon, I think people will discover the different varieties and I am sure they will like some of them. Here's to the future of honey. Okay Honey?

—Robin Pool, grade 9

Top Ten Reasons We Cry

Everybody cries. Crying is a part of human nature. If you had never cried people would think something was wrong with you. Whether we like it or not we have all cried. Crying is a way of releasing all the stress or sadness that is in your life. Sometimes we think it's embarrassing to cry in front of people so that's why most of us cry our own privacy. But really it's nothing to be ashamed of. It's simply just a way to express your feelings.

We cry when we are happy sometimes too. An example of when I started crying and I wasn't sad was when my parents came to pick me up from camp. I was sitting outside my cabin and I saw my mom and dad walking towards me and I ran up to them and give them both a hug and started crying. It wasn't because I was sad to see them it was because I was so happy I started crying and I couldn't control it. Whenever we cry I feel like it's something we can't control. Even when we are sad we don't cry on purpose. When I haven't cried in a long time sometimes I just start crying over nothing because I am making up for the times it was necessary to cry and I didn't because I was embarrassed. Crying is something that is healthy for the human mind, because it's not good to keep everything inside. It's always a relief after I cry because I've gotten rid of all that anger or sadness or whatever I'm feeling.

Crying is a natural thing for everybody. Crying embarrasses everybody, but it's not a bad thing. I consider it a good thing. It's a good way to regenerate your mind of all the bad things in your life. It always makes me feel so much better after I cry. Crying is a universal way of showing you're upset.

It's not a language anybody has to learn to understand it. Every child cried when they were born, and there is no human that hasn't cried since the day they were born. You can't learn it and it's not really anything you can fully understand. It just comes naturally.

—*Claudia Kiolbassa, grade 9*

This piece was written by a teacher using an object contributed by someone else in the room. The ending sentence makes this piece a perfect mentor text for turning the piece into a life metaphor.

Pill

It is a pill. It is cylindrical like. The outer shell is clear and the substance inside looks like the sand on the beaches of the Dominican Republic.

Its intention is to help dietary habits. It may however cause gas, bloating, diarrhea, cramping, hives, headaches, dry mouth, hair loss, nail breakage and hunger.

It is the opposite of donuts, ice cream, and cake. So many of my favorite things.

It's a type of suppressant and according to my psychiatrist any type of suppression inevitably leads to the opposite, negative effects.

These pills were once thought of as simple solutions to a difficult dilemma, now it's a way of life!

Literally it's made up of many substances. Emotionally it's made from frustration, effort, years of heartbreaking trial and error, and finally a small taste of success.

This is not really about a pill, it's about how unhappy I am when I look for outside solutions to cure my inside problems.

—*Laura Zimmer, teacher*

10 Killer Thesis: Three-in-One

If You Want Them to Develop a Thesis First

Basic Steps

1. Develop truism
2. Cast truism into a three-in-one
3. Identify the parts of this new thesis
4. Write about each part to flesh it out

Tools

- "Three-in-One Infoshots: Try It!" sheet
- "Analogy Patterns for Infoshots" sheet (in appendix)

Setting the Scene

Your students have just finished reading a piece of literature, and now you'd like for them to write about what they have read. Let's say you've just finished reading *Julius Caesar,* and you're wishing to avoid a group of essays with thesis statements like "betrayal is a bad thing" or "bad people betray their friends." While you can agree with those statements, you'd really like to show students how to create something a little more interesting, more complex, more thought-provoking, and less painful to read.

The Point

Students don't have to be naturally complex or insightful in order to think their way into a wonderfully complex and insightful statement. It can happen in simple, concrete steps. You'll need to begin with something as plain and visualizable as French toast in order to work your way to something as abstract and complex as betrayal. As my friend Jody

Giles says, "You can't get to the betrayal without the French toast." Glance at the following betrayal examples to see where we're headed here, and then read on below to see how we get there.

Teaching It

(Distribute the "Analogy Patterns for Infoshots" sheet to each student, to have near them as they write on their own paper.)

- "Students, today we're going to try something. First, think about your most recent meal. Was it breakfast? Lunch? Think about all of the different items of food or drink that you could name that were part of that meal. It might be corn on the cob, it might be French toast, it might be watermelon."

- "We're going to look at something called a three-in-one infoshot." *(Show students the examples from student samples on a document camera or overhead.)*

- "Do you see how these students were talking about one food item? They used the pattern sentences from the same sheet you have." *(Make sure students see where the sentences came from.)*

- "Next the students combined the three sentences into one sentence." *(Read the three examples.)*

- "Now it's your turn." *(Distribute "try it" sheet.)* "At the top of the page, write down your food item. Now take a few minutes to write three pattern sentences. You could put your food in either blank in the sentence. These are called 'obvious infoshots.'" *(Give them a few quiet minutes.)*

- "Now combine those three sentences into one sentence. See if you can hide the words from the pattern sentences the way the student writers did. These are called 'sneaky infoshots' and you create them by writing three sentences, then combining them into one."

(Give them writing time and then share the results.)

Figure 10–1 Analogy Patterns

Figure 10–2 Three-in-One Infoshots: Try It!

Debriefing

- "Are all of the three sentences true?"
- "How did you choose which three to write? Which to leave out?"

What to Do Next

- Instead of using a food word for a three-in-one, use an abstract term (like *friendship* or *grief*). Listen to what the combined sentences say.
- Share with students how the three-in-one can begin all kinds of pieces of writing. *(Share the betrayal examples by Lorraine Young.)*

Student Samples

▶ **THREE-IN-ONE INFOSHOTS**

Write sentences using the template patterns. Then combine them to create "sneaky infoshots."

Three   Corn on the cob can be described as barbecue's best friend.

Corn on the cob is the opposite of corn on the log.

Corn on the cob changes my flossing routine.

One   Corn on the cob: barbecue's bff, the opposite of corn on the log, oh, and it changes my flossing routine entirely.

—Eileen S., grade 8

Three   French toast is the opposite of a hamburger.

French toast can be described as amazingness.

French toast changes lives!

One   As opposed to a hamburger, the amazing French toast can definitely change your life.

—Batya K., grade 8

Three   Watermelons can cause extreme melony taste.

Watermelons can be described as green, big fruit.

Watermelon is part of my garden.

One   The big, green fruit we call a watermelon, while causing extreme melony taste, grows great in your garden.

—Sylvan G., grade 8

Three	Affection is the opposite of mean.
	Affection towards others can cause happiness.
	Affection is a type of way to show you love and appreciate someone.
One	Whenever you show someone affection, you're showing that person that you love them and appreciate them. It will bring that person happiness because they feel appreciated.

—*Tori Shiver, grade 6*

Three	Handsomeness can cause people to like you.
	Handsomeness can be described as good looking.
	Handsomeness is almost the same as beautiful.
One	Have you ever looked at someone and thought they were attractive? You probably thought they were handsome, or good looking. That's why you liked them.

—*Phillip Kaplan, grade 6*

The following examples were contributed by Lorraine Young, a Houston-area curriculum coach. Instead of beginning with a concrete item like French toast, she started with a truism for her three-in-one work. The results? She discovered that infoshots sentences can combine into powerful thesis statements for every kind of writing.

Three	Betrayal can cause chaos.
	Betrayal is part of life.
	Betrayal transforms friends into enemies
One	Betrayal is part of life that can transform friends into enemies and throw lives into chaos.

▶ AS A RESPONSE TO LITERATURE

Betrayal is part of life that can transform friends into enemies and throw lives into chaos. Just ask Brutus. Worried that his friend and emperor, Julius Caesar, was being worshiped more as a god than a man, he put into place a scheme that would nearly bring down his beloved Rome.

Three-in-One Infoshots: Try It!

Write sentences using the template patterns. Then combine them to create "sneaky infoshots."

Three	French toast is the opposite of hamburgers.
	French toast can be described as amazingness.
	French toast changes lives!
One	As opposed to a hamburger, the amazing French toast can definitely change your life.
	—Batya K., grade 8

Try it!

Three	1. _____
	_____
	_____
	2. _____
	_____
	_____
	3. _____
	_____
	_____

| One | |
| | |

Figure 10–3 Three-in-One Infoshots: Try It!

Three	Betrayal can cause chaos.
	Betrayal can turn into a lie.
	~~Betrayal transforms a naive child into a disbeliever.~~
One	Betrayal can take the form of a lie, a lie that can transform a naive child into a disbeliever and throw her life into chaos.

▶ NARRATIVE

Betrayal can take the form of a lie, a lie that can transform a naive child into a disbeliever and throw her life into chaos. I learned that lesson when I was ten years old. My world came crashing down when I discovered there was no Santa! It all started late one snowy Christmas Eve.

Three	Betrayal can cause chaos.
	Betrayal can turn into a lie.
	Betrayal transforms a naive child into a disbeliever.
One	Betrayal can take the form of a lie, a lie that can transform a naive child into a disbeliever and throw her life into chaos.

▶ PERSUASIVE

Betrayal can take the form of a lie, a lie that can transform a naive child into a disbeliever and throw her life into chaos. I learned that lesson when I was ten years old. My world came crashing down when I discovered there was no Santa! The bottom line: A lie is a lie, and parents shouldn't do it!

Three	Betrayal can cause chaos.
	Betrayal can turn into a lie.
	Betrayal can be a gift to a child.
One	When you think of betrayal and lies, you think of chaos and disappointment in a person's life, but sometimes a lie can be a magical gift to a child.

▶ **INFORMATIVE**

When you think of betrayal and lies, you think of chaos and disappointment in a person's life, but sometimes a lie can be a magical gift to a child. Is lying always a bad thing? For years, my parents had spun their web of deceit, until one day I discovered there was no Santa! Once I got over the shock of it all, I was happy I had all of those magical years believing in that jolly, fat man and his reindeer. If you're like me and have younger brothers and sisters who are still believers, you may need a few tips to keep up the ruse because, oh yeah, now you're part of that web!

Book Report Essays

If You Want Them to Write an Essay About a Book They've Read (or Any Literature)

Basic Steps

1. Read book
2. Choose aspect of book
3. Choose structure
4. Write/share kernel essay
5. Flesh out kernel into a detailed essay

Tools

- Text structure choices
- Book report essay planning sheet

Setting the Scene

Students have been reading something: short pieces or longer, all the same or different, self-selected pieces. You need to assess this somehow, but the idea of tests and multiple-choice quizzes for their reading leaves you feeling off somehow. You would really rather hear what they actually think about what they've been reading, what they notice, and how they process that.

The Point

Students could be using text structures and kernel essays to discuss their reactions to their reading. The resulting essays are unique and interesting to read, and students consider them more interesting (and easy) to write.

Teaching It

(Distribute the book report assignment sheet.)

- "Students, you have been reading your books, and most of you have finished reading. It's time to work on your essay about your book. In the past, what have your book reports looked like?" *(Listen to their answers: plot retellings, book cover designs, posters, Accelerated Reader quizzes, cereal boxes, etc.)*

- "Those are all interesting, and today I'm going to help you get started writing an essay based on your book. This essay will count as your book report."

- "First, on this sheet, write the title and author of your book."

- "Second, answer the top question: what's the best thing about your book? Maybe you liked the setting; maybe you really liked the way one of the characters talked; maybe the story got you. What was it that you liked most? Write your answer. It doesn't need to be a complete sentence."

Figure 11–1 Book report assignment sheet

- "Next, take about five minutes and summarize the story. You have only a little room, so tell the story—beginning, middle, and end—in a summary. You won't have space to do justice to the details."

- "Finished? Okay, now, here is where the book report changes into an essay. You're not going to retell your book any more than you already have in the summary. Instead, you're going to look at what you said was the best thing about the book. You'll decide what exactly you'd like to focus on, from your book, choose a structure, write a kernel essay, and then flesh it out with details from the book. Does that make sense?"

- "Let's look at some of the suggested text structures you might find useful. Say you chose 'the story of my thinking,' the structure would ask for one thing the character used to think, and then something that happened, and what the character thinks now. This, with details, will be your whole essay."

- "But if you chose the next one, you focus on one moment in that character's life. You'll tell where he or she was that moment, what happened first, next, last, and then what life lesson he or she got from it. If you chose this structure, this would be your whole essay."

- "Who has questions?"

Debriefing

- "Which structure did you choose? How did you choose that one?"
- "Are you allowed to change any of the structures?" *(Of course.)*

Name: _____

Self-Selected Reading Book Essay Assignment and Pre-Writing

What is the best thing about your book? _____

Title of book: _____

Author: _____

Plot summary: _____

_____

_____

Choose a **text structure** to talk about your book. Then write a **kernel essay** about one aspect of the book. Turn this page in for a maximum grade of B. If you would like a grade of A, then flesh out your kernel essay with details from the book, and turn in that essay with this page. The final essay should range from 400 to 700 words, typed.

Name of structure: _____
☐ ☐ ☐ ☐ ☐

Kernel essay:

1. _____

2. _____

3. _____

4. _____

5. _____

6. _____

Heard by: (three signatures) _____

_____

_____

Figure 11–2 Self-selected reading book essay assignment and pre-writing

Text Structures for Book Report

Figure 11–3 Text structures for book report

The Story of My Thinking

| What the character used to think | But this happened | So now he/she thinks |

A Memory—A Moment in the Character's Life

| Where he or she was | Moment it started | Next moment | Final moment | Truism |

Curiosity: One Thing the Character Would Like to Know About

| He/she has sometimes wondered about . . . | He/she knows that . . . | He/she also knows that . . . | But he/she can't figure out how . . . | So he/she plans to . . . |

Insight Garden/The 11-Minute Essay

| An insight about life | One illustration from literature | One illustration from a movie | An illustration from history | I wonder |

Evolution of a Term (word or phrase in the prompt)

| What the word means to the character at first | What it means to the character a little later | What the word means to the character now | How this compares to your own understanding of that word |

What to Do Next

On a planning sheet:

Select an interesting aspect of the book.

Select a structure.

Write a kernel essay.

Flesh it out with details.

Student Samples

This fourth grader used the "memory reflection" structure to talk about a play called "The Story of W.O.W."

They are inside a book mobile a bus made into a library.

Mrs. Nguyen tells Ileana that the WOW program is out of money and they will no longer have the traveling library.

Ileana has bad news about the WOW and then they thought and come up with ideas and a car wash.

They go to Uncle Carlos for help and hand out flyers for customers and Ted's barber shop, spotless cleaners and other places.

I learn that they work as a team.

—*Ryan Sanchez, grade 4*

Name __Jonah__

Due Oct. 24

SSR Book Essay Assignment and Pre-Writing

What is the best thing about your book? __The suspense and changes of the main character__

Title of book __Touching Spirit Bear__   Author __Ben Mikaelsen__

Plot summary: __He is stranded on an Alaskan Island for his latest crime. He is later mauled by the spirit bear. He is rescued and hospitalized. He is a new man of kindness through the painful experience__

Choose a text structure to talk about your book. Then write a kernel essay about one aspect of the book. Turn this page in for a maximum grade of "B." If you would like a grade of "A," then flesh out your kernel essay with details from the book, and turn in that essay with this page. The final essay should range from 400 to 700 words, typed.

Name of structure: The Story of My Thinking

| What I used to Think | But this happened | So now I think | | |

Kernel essay:

1. __Cole Matthews didnt care about anybody.__
2. __But then He was stranded and mauled on an Island.__
3. __So now he is a forgiving and gentle soul.__
4. _____
5. _____
6. _____

Heard by: (3 signatures) __Tamir__
__Brittany__
__Grace__

Figure 11–4
Jonah's planning sheet

The Story of Cole's Thinking

In Ben Mikaelsen's novel *Touching Spirit Bear,* Cole Matthews lived in Minneapolis, Minnesota. Cole didn't seem to care about anyone or anything. The reason may have been his two uncaring and nor non-compassionate parents. Cole's mom always drinks until drunk, and Cole's father beats him with his fists or a belt. Cole has been exposed to this behavior for so long it's the only way he knows to express himself. As a result, Cole has been thieving and fighting almost all his life. One of his latest crimes, smashing his classmates Peter's head against the sidewalk, gets Cole into big trouble. He now has to choose between life in prison or Circle Justice. Cole chooses circle justice and is then sent away to an Alaskan Island where he will spend the next year.

On the island he is left alone. He burns all his supplies sent from his parents because of his rage, without hesitation or regret. After several hours he finally has a little taste of loneliness and fury. He had no one to talk to, no one to trust, no one to blame, no one to yell at, and no one to be angry at.

He soon encounters the Spirit Bear. Cole attacks the bear to make it fear him but the Spirit bear fights back with painful bites and scratches. Cole has been pounced on, clawed at, the bear's teeth in his thigh, and has been thrashed at multiple times. Cole thinks that he will die from the sight of his chest, the mauling has left him with his flesh exposed from his cut open chest. He has lost all feeling in his right arm and his leg. Many of his bones have made crunching noises while being mauled.

Cole is left starving, cold, wet, badly wounded, drowning in the rain, unable to walk, throwing up, and lonely. It is one of the worst feelings in the world. Cole is struggling to survive and hanging from a thread to life. Just then the Spirit bear appears. The Spirit Bear calmly walked up to Cole and Cole had slowly reached for the bear hesitantly, but the bear seemed harmless. Cole finally touched the Spirit Bear, Cole felt it's heartbeat, its soft white fur, its warm body. Cole also felt trust for the first time.

Through that emotionally warming event in Cole's life, he finally realized he can trust and that trust doesn't come through fear. He also learned that every living thing has value and meaning. Cole is soon rescued from the Island and hospitalized. Six months later he is healed and begins to walk the earth as a forgiving and gentle soul.

—Jonah Katzman, grade 6

Name ___Ilan___

SSR Book Essay Assignment and Pre-Writing

What is the best thing about your book? ___It talks about sports.___

Title of book ___Heart of a Champion___ Author ___Carl Deuser___

Plot summary: ___Jimmy is a kid who loves and is a master at baseball, and Seth wishes he was. When Jimmy recieves a heart-breaking loss, both of them learn to have the Heart of a champion. But as Jimmy's alchohol problem grows, he is caught in an accident, and dies. But Jimmy must move on, and get past it.___

Choose a text structure to talk about your book. Then write a kernel essay about one aspect of the book. Turn this page in for a maximum grade of "B." If you would like a grade of "A," then flesh out your kernel essay with details from the book, and turn in that essay with this page. The final essay should range from 400 to 700 words, typed.

Name of structure: A Memory - a Moment in the Character's life.

| Where they were | Moment it Started | Next Moment | Final Moment | Truism |

Kernel essay:

1. Jimmy and Seth were at Tustin's shack.
2. Tustin offeres Seth and Jimmy some bear.
3. Seth wants to take one, and reaches out to take one.
4. Jimmy tells Tustin he doesn't want, and tells Seth not
4.5. to have one, so he doesn't.
6. At a young age, nobody should be drinking bear.

Heard by: (3 signatures) Kerry Bonsino, ariane Bonsino, Moriah Bonino

Figure 11-5
Ilan's planning sheet

Tustin's Shack

In *Heart of a Champion,* by Carl Deuker, as usual, Jimmy and Seth are playing baseball at Henry Ford Baseball Field. They set up a pickup game with some of their friends, including Tustin. Tustin is the oldest kid playing. Jimmy and Seth don't really like Tustin because he always makes the game unfair, he always makes the wrong calls. Seth knew that somebody had to stand up to him and make the games fair again. So finally, Seth stands up to Tustin and both of them throw a few pushes, punches, kicks and shoves. Finally, Seth wins the fight and Tustin leaves the fields. And all of the other players clap and are so happy. But after the game, Tustin comes back and tells Seth that because he beat him in the fight, he and Jimmy can come and hang out at his shack.

When Jimmy and Seth get to Tustin's shack, they notice that it is made out of old wood and it is run down and rusty. Tustin goes to the refrigerator and pulls out a bucket of ice cold beer. He also offered them some dirty magazines. Tustin asks them if they want any. Seth said, "Sounds Good." So he reached out to take out, but Jimmy would not stand for this and he would protect his friend.

Jimmy interrupts and said, "No Thanks." He also tells Tustin that Seth doesn't want any either. Seth is really angry at Jimmy, and he tells him that it would only be one beer, but Jimmy would not let Seth start drinking beer. Jimmy again also speaks for Seth again, and tells Tustin that they don't want any of his dirty magazines. Tustin said that they're missing out on a lot of fun. Then, Jimmy and Seth leave his shack. After Seth realizes that Jimmy was just looking out for him, and thanks him for protecting him.

I believe that at a young age, nobody should be drinking beer, because bad habits start early. So, if a small kid like Seth starts to drink beer at a young age, they will most likely, have a drinking problem as an adult. Then, it will be extremely hard to get rid of, and maybe, they might never be able to get rid of it. So I believe, that this is a very true truism.

—*Ilan Sonsino, grade 6*

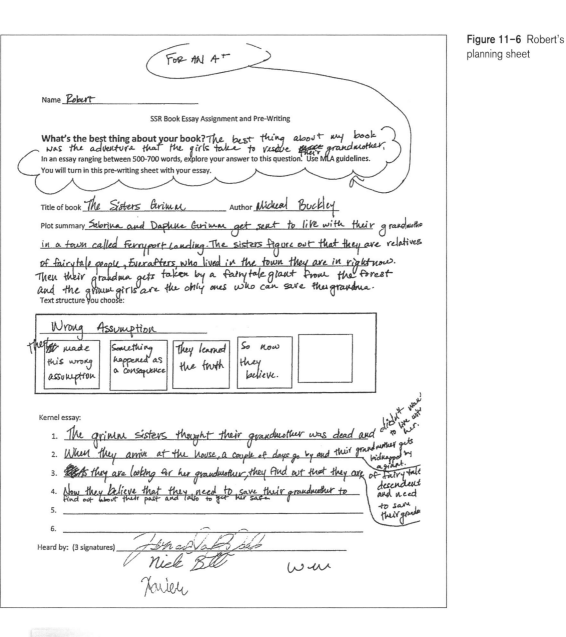

Figure 11–6 Robert's planning sheet

Wrong Assumption

In life some people make wrong choices or assumptions about things and then when they find out the truth, most of the time, something bad usually happens to them or you, well at least that is from my experience. In *The Sisters Grimm* Sabrina and Daphne Grimm live in foster homes and when they find out that they have to go live with there grandmother in Fairyport Landing. They don't want to because they thought that she was dead and they don't know anything about her. When they arrive in Fairyport Landing and they move into their grandmother's house, they find out that she is no ordinary grandmother and that they are going to be in one hell of a ride.

Sabrina and Daphne Grimm arrived in Fairyport Landing and it was wet and damp. They already hated that place. They got off the plane and their driver drove them to what they thought was their dead grandmothers' house, but really she was alive. They stayed with her for a week or so and that's when weird things started to happen. They weren't allowed to go up into a room in the attic and they were fine with it until weird noises started to come from it. After another few days went by, the noises went away and they just when they thought that they could ask their grandma what was up there, she vanished. A giant came into the home and kidnapped the Grimm sisters' grandma and ran into the woods right outside of their house.

The sisters didn't know what to do at first, but then they realized that they had to go in the woods after the giant and try to rescue their grandma. On their journey to find their grandma they realized that the forest they went into seemed magical and that there were magical things in it. They then were approached by magical creatures who told them that they were decedents of the Brothers Grimm, a fairytale family, and that they were fairytales also. They knew right then that they had to save their grandmother from the giant because they would have to get all the secrets from her just in case she were to die.

Days and weeks went past before they saw any signs of finding their grandma. They found little things, like her shoes and ripped up parts of her skirt, that lead them on a trail to find her grandmother. They wanted to give up right when they heard mumbling in the forest and looked up to see their grandmother dangling from a tree. They quickly cut her down and ran off back towards the house, but of course the giant saw them running away and chased them all the way back to the house. They were halfway from the house still in the forest when they lost the giant and escaped out of the forest and safely got back to the house.

The sisters made a mistake about their grandmother and because of that, karma hit them and something happened to her. Never make the wrong assumption about someone until you meet him or her.

—Robert Schuler, grade 9

12 Content Areas

If You Want Them to Use These Skills for Other Content

Basic Steps

1. Figure out structures to match required piece
2. Try out those structures as kernels
3. Flesh out if required for situation

Tools

- Science fair abstract planning sheet
- "Informative Text Structures" sheet

Setting the Scene

Your students are struggling with writing their science fair papers or they are trying to digest what they have been learning in American history. You don't see them transferring what they have been learning about structures to other academic content. You suspect they could use a little help crossing that bridge.

The Point

Text structures and kernel essays can help students show what they know when they are confronted with other academic situations.

Teaching It

- "Students, what have you been studying?" *(Listen.)* "The American Revolution? Okay, so today we're going to write about that! Pick out one part that you find most fascinating." *(Listen to ideas . . . "the Boston Tea Party?" "the signing of the Declaration?")*

- "Great!" *(Distribute the "Informative Text Structures" sheet.)* "Everyone choose a structure from these choices. Try your hand at writing a kernel essay about that time in history. Would you like to see an example?" *(Show them one.)*

(Give them time to write and then share.)

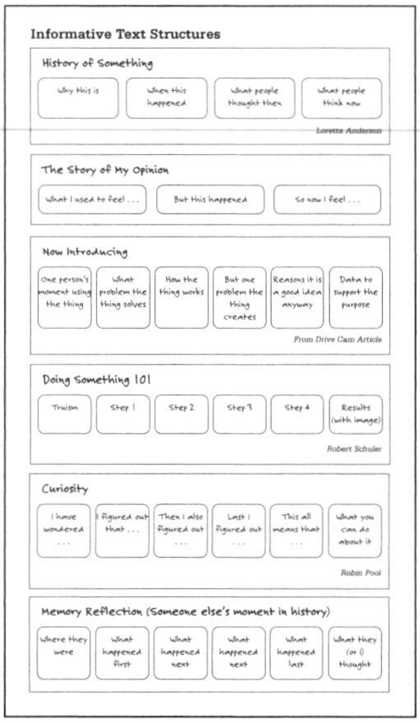

Figure 12–1 Informative text structures

Debriefing

- "Can you imagine using this process to show what you know about other kinds of learning?"

What to Do Next

On a planning sheet:

Select a topic.

Select a structure.

Write a kernel essay.

Flesh it out with details.

Spin-offs

Use text structures and kernel essays to help students write science fair background research, abstracts, or reports about anything they are studying. The student samples give examples of these.

Informative Text Structures

Figure 12–2
"Informative Text
Structures" sheet

History of Something

| Why this is | When this happened | What people thought then | What people think now |

Loretta Anderson

The Story of My Opinion

| What I used to feel ... | But this happened | So now I feel ... |

Now Introducing

| One person's moment using the thing | What problem the thing solves | How the thing works | But one problem the thing creates | Reasons it is a good idea anyway | Data to support the purpose |

From Drive Cam Article

Doing Something 101

| Truism | Step 1 | Step 2 | Step 3 | Step 4 | Results (with image) |

Robert Schuler

continues

Figure 12–2
"Informative Text
Structures" sheet,
continued

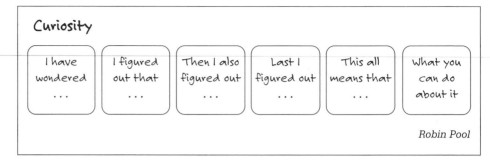

Curiosity

| I have wondered . . . | I figured out that . . . | Then I also figured out . . . | Last I figured out . . . | This all means that . . . | What you can do about it |

Robin Pool

Memory Reflection (Someone else's moment in history)

| Where they were | What happened first | What happened next | What happened next | What happened last | What they (or I) thought |

Student Samples

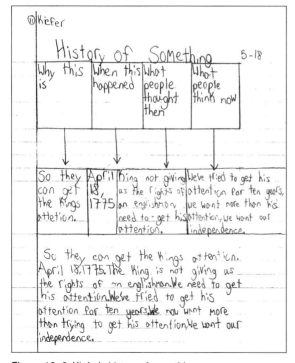

Figure 12–3 Kiefer's history of something

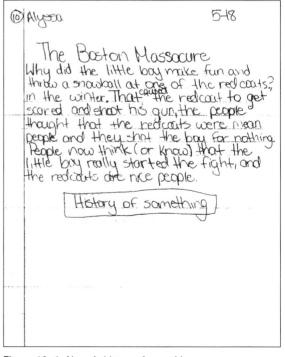

Figure 12–4 Alyssa's history of something

⑫ Arron   5-18

George Washington
Some people think...
George Washington was a bad leader during
war. that people told him to prove
that he can win a battle.

Other people think....
That George washington is a nice
leader that would fight for them.
George washington won the battle the
battle against the british.

But I think....
Washington was a great leader
and fight for his wife and do what is
best for his life. and do what is right.
and must be made.

What tells me is....
That washington was a good
man trying to get freedom hoping for
acting a leader for land and freedom

"Comparing Notes"

Figure 12–5 Arron's comparing notes

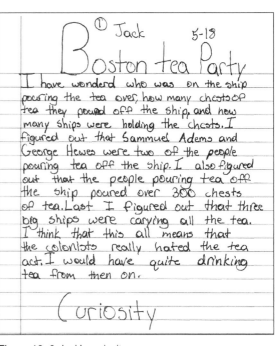

① Jack   5-18
Boston tea Party
I have wonderd who was on the ship
pouring the tea over, how many chests of
tea they poured off the ship, and how
many ships were holding the chests. I
figured out that Sammuel Adems and
George Hewes were two of the people
pouring tea off the ship. I also figured
out that the people pouring tea off
the ship poured over 300 chests
of tea. Last I figured out that three
big ships were carying all the tea.
I think that this all means that
the colonists really hated the tea
act. I would have quite drinking
tea from then on.

Curiosity

Figure 12–6 Jack's curiosity

⑭ Lexie   5-18

Comparing Notes (Mine & Others)

Two Sides of a coin

Some people think that they should
stay loyal to Great Brittan and
their king. While Others think that
they should separate, from Great Brittan
and govern themselves. I think that
people should be allowed to think what
they want to. That tells me that
everyone has a different opinion on
things.

Figure 12–7 Lexie's comparing notes

Name: _____

Science Fair Project Abstract

Put your **title here**

_____

_____

Text structure: **Science Fair Abstract**

what question you are answering (your problem)	what you suspected was true (your hypothesis)	what you did (your steps, or experiment procedure)	what happened (your results)	what that means (your conclusion)	

Write your **kernel essay** here.

1. _____

2. _____

3. _____

4. _____

5. _____

6. _____

Create your **abstract** like this

Paragraph 1: sentences 1 and 2.

Paragraph 2: your steps.

Paragraph 3: sentences 4 and 5.

Figure 12–8 Science fair project abstract

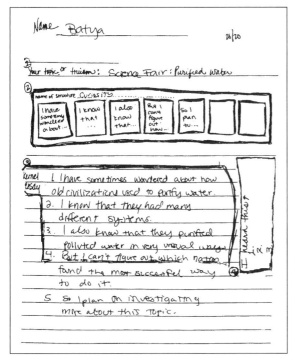

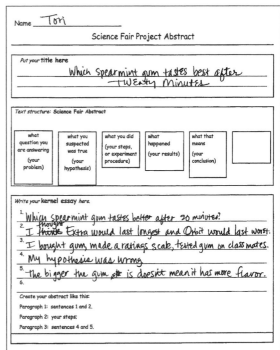

Figure 12–9 Batya's science fair sheet   **Figure 12–10** Tori's science fair sheet

▶ **ABSTRACT**

Which Spearmint Flavored Gum Tastes the Best After Twenty Minutes?

My question was which spearmint gum tastes the best after twenty minutes. My hypothesis was that the brand, Extra would last the longest and that the orbit would last the worst. The reason for my hypothesis is because on the package of the Extra it says long lasting gum and because orbit is small and does not look like it can hold-much taste.

I began my experiment by buying the gum necessary for this project. After that I made the gum scales for my classmates and myself to rate the gum taste. Then my classmates and I tested the gum. We chewed for the necessary twenty minutes I then handed out the scales. We rated the left over on the scale of one to five [one being the lowest and five being the highest].

After all the testing was over I found my hypothesis to be very incorrect Trident had gotten the highest scores with no one under four and Extra getting the least being the only brand with a one from the scale and nothing higher than a four. This proves even the bigger the strip or piece of gum does not mean that it has more flavor.

—*Tori Shiver, grade 6*

13 Extracting Structures from Great Pieces

If You Want Them to Use the Moves of Other Writers

Basic Steps

1. Read a piece
2. Chunk it
3. Summarize each chunk
4. Cast into text structure
5. Try out the structure with other content

Tools

- "Drive Cam" article
- Declaration of Independence example
- *Hamlet* example
- Text structures from great pieces

Setting the Scene

You have been using text structures created just for the students' writing. Now you would like for your students to get a different feel for the moves that writers make. In fact, you'd like for them to use moves made by some famous writers. You might want them to capture a structure in something they are reading, or you might want to lead them to blindly use a structure before you show them which great piece it came from.

The Point

As far back as the Renaissance, teachers have had students practice imitating form or content. The students looked at what we now call "mentor text" and rewrote the content into a different form or filled the form with different content.

It's fun both to capture text structures from great pieces and fill those structures with content from the students' lives. We will do both here. First we'll have students capture a structure for use; then we'll have them use that structure to fill in with their own content. The following example comes from *Texts and Lessons for Content-Area Reading* (Daniels and Steineke 2011).

Teaching It

- "Today we're going to capture a structure. Let's read this article." *(Read, and then assign students to groups.)*
- "Now each group will be assigned one paragraph. Read your paragraph and together write a summary for that paragraph." *(Give them time and then listen to the summary sentences in sequence.)*

After the students leave, convert the sentences to more general words, and put them into boxes. Name the structure and post it for students to choose when they next need a structure.

Figure 13–1 "Drive Cam" article

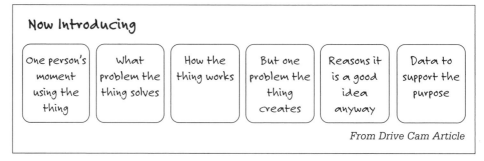

Figure 13–2 "Now Introducing . . ." text structure

What to Do Next

On a planning sheet:

- Select a topic.
- Select a structure.
- Write a kernel essay.
- Flesh it out with details.

Figure 13–3 Planning sheet

Student Samples

Figure 13–4 Rebecca's planning sheet

Figure 13–5 Rebecca's essay

Spin-offs

You can lead students through a structure (like the "Dilemma" structure). Have them think of a dilemma they are currently encountering, and then ask them to write one sentence per box for that structure. Write and share. Then uncover the original text that supplied the structure (for instance, the Hamlet speech for the dilemma structure). It's fun!

The *Washington Post*

Watch your driving, kids. The parents are watching.

By **Matt Zapotosky**
Oct. 26, 2008

WASHINGTON — Ken Richardson does not have to ride in his 17-year-old daughter's Ford Escort to know when she takes a turn too fast. The camera system installed in her car will e-mail him about it.

The cameras are among the latest tools in the struggle to reduce teen car crashes, a problem that has been particularly vexing in Maryland. Last year, crashes involving drivers ages 16 to 20 killed 112 people in the state. Such accidents are often caused not by alcohol or overt recklessness but by simple driver inexperience. The problem has persisted despite efforts by lawmakers to restrict teen driving privileges.

The camera, mounted on the front windshield, captures footage of what is happening outside as well as in the vehicle. It saves about 20 seconds of that footage only when its sensors are triggered by unusual driving maneuvers such as sudden braking or swerving. Saved footage is transmitted back to DriveCam via a cellular network. DriveCam experts review the videos, add tips for the young drivers and post them to a Web site. Parents receive an e-mail alert when the videos are posted.

The camera can capture anything going on in the car, but the company uploads only footage that involves unsafe driving. If an event is captured that is embarrassing to the

> "I feel like I'm being baby-sat, like I'm being watched constantly. It drives me nuts."

teen . . . then we're not going to return it to the family," Carpenter said.

In the month or so since the camera was installed, Richardson's daughter has not been caught on camera doing anything too bad, but the camera has been a sore point. "I feel like I'm being baby-sat, like I'm being watched constantly. It drives me nuts," said Stacie.

Richardson has tried every possible angle to convince his daughter that the camera is a good idea. He has tried telling her she could earn new driving privileges by avoiding major incidents. He has appealed to her sense of benevolence, telling her that being a part of the study could save others' lives. And he has tried telling her that when she gets older, she'll want the same kind of device for her kids.

The limited research conducted on Drive-Cam elsewhere in the country seems to support her dad. DriveCam tracked 25 new drivers using the camera and feedback system for more than a year starting in 2006. The six people who triggered the camera most frequently in the beginning, did so 86 percent less later on.

Figure 13–6 Washington Post "Drive Cam" article

The Washington Post

Watch your driving, kids. The parents are watching.

By **Matt Zapotosky**
Oct. 26, 2008

one scenario using the thing

WASHINGTON — Ken Richardson does not have to ride in his 17-year-old daughter's Ford Escort to know when she takes a turn too fast. The camera system installed in her car will e-mail him about it.

What problem this thing Solves

The cameras are among the latest tools in the struggle to reduce teen car crashes, a problem that has been particularly vexing in Maryland. Last year, crashes involving drivers ages 16 to 20 killed 112 people in the state. Such accidents are often caused not by alcohol or overt recklessness but by simple driver inexperience. The problem has persisted despite efforts by lawmakers to restrict teen driving privileges.

how it works

The camera, mounted on the front windshield, captures footage of what is happening outside as well as in the vehicle. It saves about 20 seconds of that footage only when its sensors are triggered by unusual driving maneuvers such as sudden braking or swerving. Saved footage is transmitted back to DriveCam via a cellular network. DriveCam experts review the videos, add tips for the young drivers and post them to a Web site. Parents receive an e-mail alert when the videos are posted.

what it doesn't do

The camera can capture anything going on in the car, but the company uploads only footage that involves unsafe driving. If an event is captured that is embarrassing to the

"I feel like I'm being baby-sat, like I'm being watched constantly. It drives me nuts."

teen . . . then we're not going to return it to the family," Carpenter said.

BUT HERE is one problem the thing Creates

In the month or so since the camera was installed, Richardson's daughter has not been caught on camera doing anything too bad, but the camera has been a sore point. "I feel like I'm being baby-sat, like I'm being watched constantly. It drives me nuts," said Stacie.

Reasons the thing is a good idea

Richardson has tried every possible angle to convince his daughter that the camera is a good idea. He has tried telling her she could earn new driving privileges by avoiding major incidents. He has appealed to her sense of benevolence, telling her that being a part of the study could save others' lives. And he has tried telling her that when she gets older, she'll want the same kind of device for her kids.

Data to support the effectiveness

The limited research conducted on DriveCam elsewhere in the country seems to support her dad. DriveCam tracked 25 new drivers using the camera and feedback system for more than a year starting in 2006. The six people who triggered the camera most frequently in the beginning, did so 86 percent less later on.

Figure 13–7 "Drive Cam" article with notes

Rebecca chose the "Now Introducing . . ." structure to discuss a new literary form. She wrote her kernel essay and then detailed it.

Name **Rebecca**

Planning Sheet

Type of Writing (Check One)

☐ Writing about myself ☐ Writing to inform me ☑ Writing to inform others ☐ Writing to persuade ☐ Writing about literature

Put your truism *(aka assertion aka problem here aka main question)* **here**

Homestuck just might get people reading again.

Put your text structure here. Now Introducing...

| One scenario using the thing | What problem the thing solves | How it works | But One problem it creates | Reason it's a good idea anyway | Data to support the thing |

Write your kernel essay here.

1. What if teens and adults alike read again?
2. Homestuck makes people who hate reading read. (That's a problem solver.)
3. It works just like a book but has music and games.
4. Entirely web-based, sort of confusing, it takes up a lot of your time.
5. But it's a great, well thought-out and fun story.
6. As results prove, everyone seems to find something enjoyable about it.

Plan for details:

Action Detail

☐ snapshots   ☐ sensory details
☐ thoughtshots ☐ ba-da-bing
☐ dialogue   ☐ _____

Infoshots

☐ description   ☐ synonyms/antonyms
☐ compare/contrast ☐ part/whole
☐ cause/effect   ☐ item/category
☐ before/after   ☐ _____

Figure 13–8 Rebecca's planning sheet

A Whole New Way

Are you a reluctant reader? Most people nowadays are. Especially teenagers. We hate reading. Because of that our next generation seems to be declining in intelligence and creativity. People, not just youth, would prefer getting into their favorite TV show, band, or video game over actually taking the time to read a good story. So what if it was possible to combine animation, music, and video games all into a graphic novel format? That could possibly be the next best thing to help get people reading again.

Well I'm glad to introduce this brand new type of media that is known as a webcomic! Now most webcomics are known to be just short little updateable comic strips with some funny punch-line at the end. But there's one comic in particular I'd like to focus on, and it's one that's a full out story with all sorts of media to help it along. This whole new way of thinking is called Homestuck, and is free to read online over at www.mspaintadventures.com. It works just like a book in most ways. Flip the page, read everything that's on it, and then repeat. Easy, right? The only huge difference is occasionally you'll run into a cool flash animation with music, or to an interactive fight scene, or even a pixilated game. But everything it does is just to provide depth and uniqueness to the plot and characters. Also just to keep things exciting.

Of course there are cons to things this awesome. One huge flaw that people seem to run into is the fact that it's entirely web based story, so there's not always access to it, and it may not be easy to use if you're new to a computer. Another is, Homestuck has a very odd way of telling itself. It's told almost completely in second person, and uses very heavy vocabulary. So it might be confusing to a new reader.

Nevertheless, it is an amazing, well thought-out story with a great plot; don't let the art fool you. One of the best things in my opinion is its length; it is very long, leaving plenty of time for dark twists, grieving, humor, character development, and temporary mood and style changes. I also think because of the occasional mood and style changes it really forces you into the story, and helps you feel for what the characters are going through.

Recently certain tests were given. Ten very slow readers were shown this webcomic. Eight of them greatly enjoyed Homestuck for everything that it is, and the other 2 never were able to finish it. But this just proves that all these pros and cons just help to add on to this newfound, fun sub-genre's ability to keep readers reading, and on the edge of their seats. And that this might very well be the beginning of a whole new way of storytelling.

—Rebecca Onofre, grade 9

These text structures were all derived from other pieces. They are wonderful as guided kernel essays, after which the students enjoy trying to figure out where they have heard those structures before.

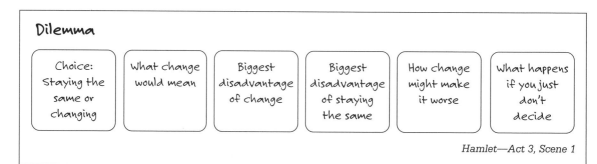

Figure 13–9 Dilemma text structure

Figure 13–10
Hamlet quote example

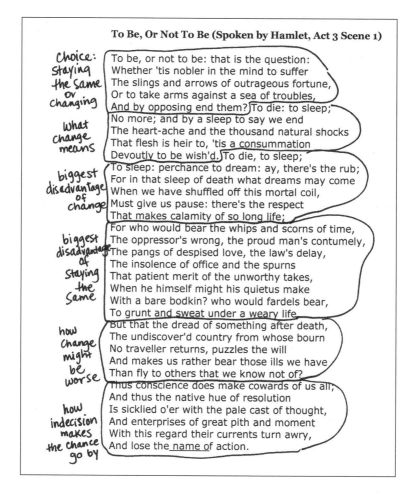

Sample kernel using "Dilemma" text structure.

1. Should I go to summer camp this summer?
2. I would have to pack my bags.
3. The biggest disadvantage to go is that it cost a lot of money.
4. If I stay home I would be bored.
5. If I don't go, Sandra and Bernardo wouldn't want to go.
6. If I don't decide summer will end.

—Tamara Marcushamer , grade 7

My Dilemma

Here is my dilemma . . .

Should I go to summer camp this summer or should I just stay home with my family? Those are my two options that I'm trying to figure out.

If I do go to summer camp this summer and not stay home I would have to start packing my bags. And start labeling my clothes so they wont get lost, which is a lot of work. I would also have to buy things I would need for summer camp. My parents would also have to enroll me to be able to go to camp.

The biggest disadvantage of going to summer camp is that it will cost a lot of money. The camp is for 21 days which would cause me to miss my parents a lot.

The biggest disadvantage of staying home and not going to summer camp would be that it would be tedious at home and I would be very lazy, which will ruin my summer vacation.

If my brother and sister, Sandra and Bernardo do not want to go to summer camp it will ruin every thing! Because then I would be alone and won't have my best friends with me. I would also miss both of them a lot, and if they do not go I would have to miss even more people!

If I never decide whether I want to go to summer camp this summer would end and I will have to wait for next summer. And probably by then I would have the same dilemma like this one which is very hard to figure out. I do not like dilemmas at all!!

—Tamara Marcushamer, grade 7

Should I paint my room or leave it as it is now?

1. Should I paint my room and add stuff that is more me or not?
2. The change would mean my room would look different.
3. I may not even like the change.
4. I might really want to change my room.
5. What if it doesn't turn out like I plan.
6. My room might never change if I don't decide.

—*Juliette Miller, grade 7*

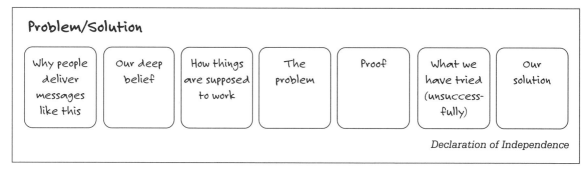

Problem/Solution

| Why people deliver messages like this | Our deep belief | How things are supposed to work | The problem | Proof | What we have tried (unsuccessfully) | Our solution |

Declaration of Independence

Figure 13–11 Problem/Solution, Declaration of Independence

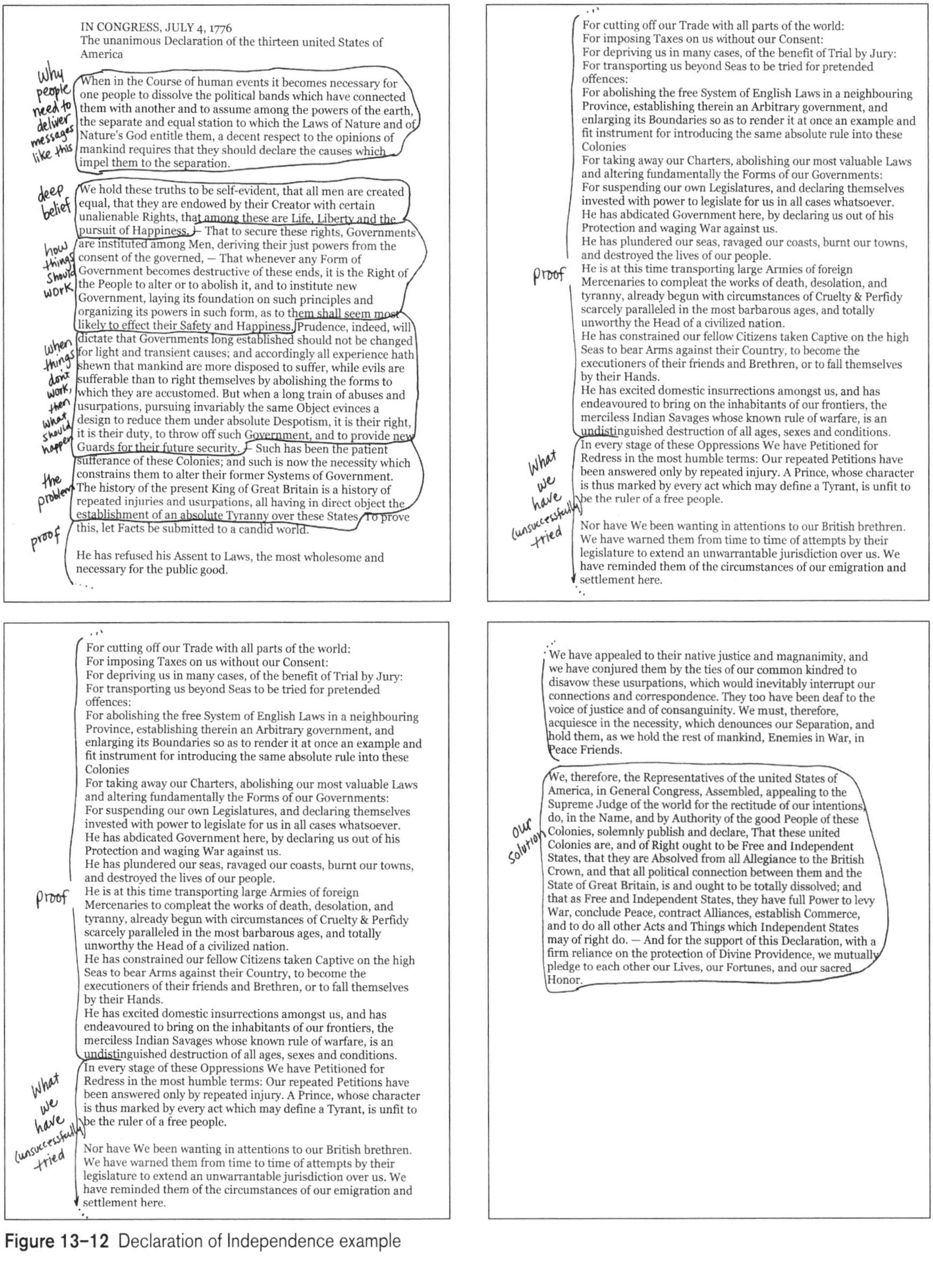

[handwritten annotation: Why people need to deliver messages like this]

IN CONGRESS, JULY 4, 1776
The unanimous Declaration of the thirteen united States of America

When in the Course of human events it becomes necessary for one people to dissolve the political bands which have connected them with another and to assume among the powers of the earth, the separate and equal station to which the Laws of Nature and of Nature's God entitle them, a decent respect to the opinions of mankind requires that they should declare the causes which impel them to the separation.

[handwritten annotation: deep belief]

[handwritten annotation: how things should work]

[handwritten annotation: when things don't work, then what should happen]

[handwritten annotation: the problem]

We hold these truths to be self-evident, that all men are created equal, that they are endowed by their Creator with certain unalienable Rights, that among these are Life, Liberty and the pursuit of Happiness.— That to secure these rights, Governments are instituted among Men, deriving their just powers from the consent of the governed, — That whenever any Form of Government becomes destructive of these ends, it is the Right of the People to alter or to abolish it, and to institute new Government, laying its foundation on such principles and organizing its powers in such form, as to them shall seem most likely to effect their Safety and Happiness. Prudence, indeed, will dictate that Governments long established should not be changed for light and transient causes; and accordingly all experience hath shewn that mankind are more disposed to suffer, while evils are sufferable than to right themselves by abolishing the forms to which they are accustomed. But when a long train of abuses and usurpations, pursuing invariably the same Object evinces a design to reduce them under absolute Despotism, it is their right, it is their duty, to throw off such Government, and to provide new Guards for their future security.— Such has been the patient sufferance of these Colonies; and such is now the necessity which constrains them to alter their former Systems of Government. The history of the present King of Great Britain is a history of repeated injuries and usurpations, all having in direct object the establishment of an absolute Tyranny over these States. To prove this, let Facts be submitted to a candid world.

[handwritten annotation: proof]

He has refused his Assent to Laws, the most wholesome and necessary for the public good.

. . .

For cutting off our Trade with all parts of the world:
For imposing Taxes on us without our Consent:
For depriving us in many cases, of the benefit of Trial by Jury:
For transporting us beyond Seas to be tried for pretended offences:
For abolishing the free System of English Laws in a neighbouring Province, establishing therein an Arbitrary government, and enlarging its Boundaries so as to render it at once an example and fit instrument for introducing the same absolute rule into these Colonies
For taking away our Charters, abolishing our most valuable Laws and altering fundamentally the Forms of our Governments:
For suspending our own Legislatures, and declaring themselves invested with power to legislate for us in all cases whatsoever.
He has abdicated Government here, by declaring us out of his Protection and waging War against us.
He has plundered our seas, ravaged our coasts, burnt our towns, and destroyed the lives of our people.

[handwritten annotation: proof]

He is at this time transporting large Armies of foreign Mercenaries to compleat the works of death, desolation, and tyranny, already begun with circumstances of Cruelty & Perfidy scarcely paralleled in the most barbarous ages, and totally unworthy the Head of a civilized nation.
He has constrained our fellow Citizens taken Captive on the high Seas to bear Arms against their Country, to become the executioners of their friends and Brethren, or to fall themselves by their Hands.
He has excited domestic insurrections amongst us, and has endeavoured to bring on the inhabitants of our frontiers, the merciless Indian Savages whose known rule of warfare, is an undistinguished destruction of all ages, sexes and conditions.

[handwritten annotation: What we have (unsuccessfully) tried]

In every stage of these Oppressions We have Petitioned for Redress in the most humble terms: Our repeated Petitions have been answered only by repeated injury. A Prince, whose character is thus marked by every act which may define a Tyrant, is unfit to be the ruler of a free people.

Nor have We been wanting in attentions to our British brethren. We have warned them from time to time of attempts by their legislature to extend an unwarrantable jurisdiction over us. We have reminded them of the circumstances of our emigration and settlement here.

. . .

For cutting off our Trade with all parts of the world:
For imposing Taxes on us without our Consent:
For depriving us in many cases, of the benefit of Trial by Jury:
For transporting us beyond Seas to be tried for pretended offences:
For abolishing the free System of English Laws in a neighbouring Province, establishing therein an Arbitrary government, and enlarging its Boundaries so as to render it at once an example and fit instrument for introducing the same absolute rule into these Colonies
For taking away our Charters, abolishing our most valuable Laws and altering fundamentally the Forms of our Governments:
For suspending our own Legislatures, and declaring themselves invested with power to legislate for us in all cases whatsoever.
He has abdicated Government here, by declaring us out of his Protection and waging War against us.
He has plundered our seas, ravaged our coasts, burnt our towns, and destroyed the lives of our people.

[handwritten annotation: proof]

He is at this time transporting large Armies of foreign Mercenaries to compleat the works of death, desolation, and tyranny, already begun with circumstances of Cruelty & Perfidy scarcely paralleled in the most barbarous ages, and totally unworthy the Head of a civilized nation.
He has constrained our fellow Citizens taken Captive on the high Seas to bear Arms against their Country, to become the executioners of their friends and Brethren, or to fall themselves by their Hands.
He has excited domestic insurrections amongst us, and has endeavoured to bring on the inhabitants of our frontiers, the merciless Indian Savages whose known rule of warfare, is an undistinguished destruction of all ages, sexes and conditions.

[handwritten annotation: What we have (unsuccessfully) tried]

In every stage of these Oppressions We have Petitioned for Redress in the most humble terms: Our repeated Petitions have been answered only by repeated injury. A Prince, whose character is thus marked by every act which may define a Tyrant, is unfit to be the ruler of a free people.

Nor have We been wanting in attentions to our British brethren. We have warned them from time to time of attempts by their legislature to extend an unwarrantable jurisdiction over us. We have reminded them of the circumstances of our emigration and settlement here.

. . .

We have appealed to their native justice and magnanimity, and we have conjured them by the ties of our common kindred to disavow these usurpations, which would inevitably interrupt our connections and correspondence. They too have been deaf to the voice of justice and of consanguinity. We must, therefore, acquiesce in the necessity, which denounces our Separation, and hold them, as we hold the rest of mankind, Enemies in War, in Peace Friends.

[handwritten annotation: Our Solution]

We, therefore, the Representatives of the united States of America, in General Congress, Assembled, appealing to the Supreme Judge of the world for the rectitude of our intentions, do, in the Name, and by Authority of the good People of these Colonies, solemnly publish and declare, That these united Colonies are, and of Right ought to be Free and Independent States, that they are Absolved from all Allegiance to the British Crown, and that all political connection between them and the State of Great Britain, is and ought to be totally dissolved; and that as Free and Independent States, they have full Power to levy War, conclude Peace, contract Alliances, establish Commerce, and to do all other Acts and Things which Independent States may of right do. — And for the support of this Declaration, with a firm reliance on the protection of Divine Providence, we mutually pledge to each other our Lives, our Fortunes, and our sacred Honor.

Figure 13–12 Declaration of Independence example

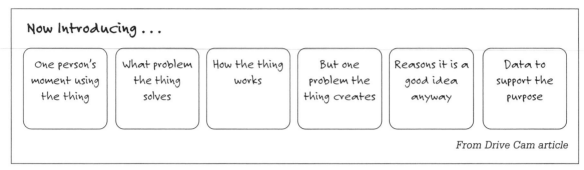

Figure 13–13 Now Introducing . . .

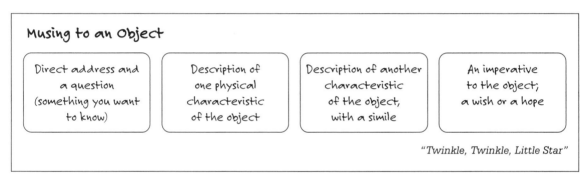

Figure 13–14 Musing to an object

Sample using "Twinkle, Twinkle, Little Star" text structure

> Can Opener, why don't you work the way you're supposed to work?
>
> Your sharp blade cuts all the way around a can, and then you become possessed!
>
> Your tiny motor purrs like a 1958 Chevy.
>
> My dear can opener, I wish you would not spit food at me when you complete your work.
>
> —Jayne Hover, teacher

At my school, students wanted to propose a solution to a problem with their noontime prayers. They wrote a group kernel essay, then divided up parts for detailing. They did not know that we were using the structure from the Declaration of Independence until after they had finished their work. They liked the structure more than a "regular" problem/solution structure. When they were ready, they delivered the proposal to the head of our school, who graciously granted their request.

Dear Ms. Oakes,

Why do students deliver messages like this?

The eighth grade students of this academy feel we should have a say in what goes on around this facility.

What deep belief do we share?

We believe that our G-d would appreciate, if he had human characteristics, us chanting the Birkat HaMazon. He provides us with food, although indirectly we should be able to thank him in a way we find suitable.

During prayers the students of the EKA should be able to express our prayers in a way we might know better. Some of us might have different beliefs or way of davining at home. And some of us would feel more comfortable praying in a way we know best.

How are things supposed to work?

We believe that a proper Birkat should include children participating and enjoying it.

What is the problem?

Children do not want to participate, nor are they enjoying it.

What is your proof?

Every day we witness kids not participating. They seem to be more interested in eating and gabbing with their friends.

To prove this, here are some facts.

> Kids are having side conversations instead of praying.
>
> The 5th and 6th graders prefer talking about Fantasy Football than thanking G-d for our food.
>
> I must admit that even we, the 8th graders, talk during the Birkat.
>
> There are many kids who don't know it because it is extremely long.
>
> None of the teachers are familiar with the tune, so they can't help us either.
>
> Ms. Bernabei doesn't speak Hebrew so she can't help out.
>
> You have asked Ms. Block to sing with us but it has failed.
>
> We still don't participate.
>
> We still eat and chat; teachers still try to make us sing.
>
> Kids do not participate at all, and there's nothing we can do about it.
>
> Maybe if we sing a different version of the Birkat HaMazon our problems will be solved.

What is the solution?

We believe that if we incorporate the Camp Young Judaea Birkat into our lunch hour, kids would participate. Now, you might be thinking, "Well I am so busy, how am I supposed to have time to make a solution to the issue at hand?" Well, Ms. Oakes, you need not worry! We, the Representatives of 6th period lunch, suggest that we replace the Birkat HaMazon, which nobody participates in, with the Camp Young Judaea version of Birkat HaMazon.

And here is our pledge: the eighth-year students of this glorious academy shall lead the new and improved Birkat every Tuesday that we are present and able to do so. We shall take it upon ourselves to teach the other lunch-goers this version of the Birkat. None of this will go haywire. We have faith in the eighth grade. We could start as soon as next Tuesday.

We look forward to hearing your reaction and hope you will consider our proposal. Thank you for your time.

Sincerely,
The Eighth Grade Class of 2011–2012
Brittany Duke
Sylvan Gurinsky
Grace Goldstein
Tamir Meishar
Eileen Stolow
Batya Katz

GLOSSARY OF TERMS

Two hands–the graphic demonstrating the two most basic kinds of text: knowledge and experience. Readers are most interested in pieces that include both kinds of text. For further reading, check Thomas Newkirk's *The School Essay Manifesto*.

Text structure–the plan, or path, that a piece will follow; it must involve at least one step from each of the two hands, above, in order to track movement of the mind, showing what you know and how you know it. Other than that one requirement, text structures can be revised in any way that works for the writing situation. These can be created intentionally by a writer or gleaned from other writers. For ease of discussion, we place these steps into sequenced boxes. For further reading, see Aristotle's *Rhetoric* and Quintilian's *Institutes of Oratory*.

Kernel essay–A writer writes about the topic, using the text structure as a guide, creating one sentence per box. These sentences are called a *kernel essay*. The next step is for the writer to read the kernel essay aloud to several listeners to see whether that structure worked for the topic. For further reading, see Gretchen Bernabei's *Reviving the Essay*.

Guided kernel essay–The teacher doesn't show the students the structure ahead of time; instead, she leads them through writing a kernel essay by phrasing each step of a structure as a question and giving them time to write an answer in one sentence. As each question is read, she draws the box for that step on the blackboard (or some other visual display), until the entire text structure is visible.

Truisms–also called thematic statements, or life lessons. These are statements that are true for most people. (This makes them debatable.) Sentences are most useful when written in third person, as general truisms about the world or about life. If students write second-person sentences, or imperative sentences, like "Don't judge other people," help them convert them to third person: "It's difficult not to judge other people," for example. If students write first-person sentences, like "I love my dog," help them convert them to third person: "People love their dogs," for example. For information about the use of maxims in classical oratory, see Aristotle's *Rhetoric*. For contemporary resources, google "truisms" or Gretchen Bernabei's *Lightning in a Bottle*.

Obvious infoshot—a sentence using the template pattern sentences from the infoshots analogy page, in order to add information to a piece of writing. (I like my dog. **My dog can be described as playful. He can be described as huge.**)

Sneaky infoshot—the use of the template pattern sentences, combined into the piece in such a way that the reader doesn't recognize the original template pattern sentences. (I like my **playful, huge** dog.)

Expanded infoshot—one template pattern sentence, explained. After the explanation is written, the original template sentence can be deleted. (~~My dog can be described as playful.~~ Whenever I come into the room, he runs up with a chew toy in his mouth, hoping for a game of catch.) For developing your own infoshots pattern sentences, google SAT analogy patterns.

Three-in-one infoshot—a two-step operation: you write three different obvious infoshots and then combine them into one sneaky infoshot. These are useful for infusing information into a piece of writing or for thesis statements. For sentence-combining practice, see Don and Jenny Killgallon's *Sentence Combining*. For powerful, focused grammatical "brushstrokes," see Harry Noden's *Image Grammar*.

Three	French toast is the opposite of hamburgers.
	French toast can be described as amazingness.
	French toast changes lives!
One	As opposed to a hamburger, the amazing French toast can definitely change your life.
	—Batya K., grade 8

Quick list of memories—the process of listing different individual short memories of different kinds, to use as an idea source for writing personal narratives. Memories should be moments, not long periods of time; the quick list asks students about specific categories (like proud moments; moments involving birds, insects, reptiles; bad hair moments; postcard moments you hope to remember). For more information, see Paula Brock's *Nudges*.

Gritty life quick list—the process of listing different kinds of (non-narrative) thoughts a person has in his or her head at any given moment, to use as an idea source for writing any kind of writing. For background pedagogy and inspiration, see James Moffett's *Teaching the Universe of Discourse*.

Indelible moment—the process of capturing a significant memory, especially through different kinds of writing paper that trigger memories and situational contexts. For the seeds of this idea, see Tom Romano's *Blending Genre, Altering Style*.

Ba-da-bing—one example of detail-combining using a sequence of icons to represent the sequence of text showing where your feet were,

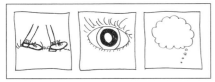

what your eye saw, and what you thought. To use the ba-da-bing for expository writing, the present tense will be more useful. *(When you walk into the store, you notice the bakery aisle and you decide to buy bread.)* For more information, see Gretchen Bernabei's *Reviving the Essay*.

TEXT ICONS

The following icons represent specific kinds of text. These can be used for details, or they can also be used to generate compositions or text structures.

Each will give an example of how to add details to the sentence: **Boys laugh.**

Icon	Type of Text	Sample Details for a Narrative (past tense)	Sample Details for Expository (present tense)
	Talking (dialogue, direct or indirect)	"Did you hear those boys chuckling?" my mom asked.	Experts agree that laughter is good for everybody.
	Thinking (inner speech or thoughtshots)	I knew it. They were laughing at me. At least that's what I suspected.	When boys laugh, they seem to attract the admiration of their peers.
	Seeing (snapshots)	I looked up and saw the three boys standing in the corner, doubled over in laughter.	When a boy laughs, his eyebrows rise, and his lips compress at first.
	Doing (active verbs)	As the boys choked with laughter, tears ran down their faces. The air hummed with humor.	Boys gather to play sports, to compete physically, and to laugh.
	Information (background or analytic)	For the first time all year, the boys from Mr. Kauffman's class laughed out loud.	The boys laugh, experiencing what researchers call a "social vocalization, which binds people together."
	Smells (literal or figurative)	I smelled the enchiladas, the sandwiches, and the embarrassment in the cafeteria as the boys shrieked with laughter.	Boys never grow too old to laugh at certain smells.
	Sounds (nonverbal sound effects)	The boys were snorting, wheezing with laughter, chortling and chuckling.	Contagious, the sounds of the boys' laughter cause everyone nearby to join in.

Icon	Type of Text	Sample Details for a Narrative (past tense)	Sample Details for Expository (present tense)
	Physical reactions (goosebumps)	My heart sank as I heard their mocking laughter.	As the boys laugh, they experience a flood of relief and relaxation.
	Emotional reactions (especially in conflict)	Although it was hilarious, I felt guilty laughing with them.	When boys laugh together, they test each other and bond strong friendships.
	Book references	The boys laughed with Grinchlike delight as they threw the paper around the room.	Sometimes the laughter of boys can be intimidating, especially when they are in Grinchlike moods.
	Movie references	Suddenly they all laughed a tittering, timid, Munchkin kind of laugh.	One kind of laughter is timid, shy Munchkin-like laughter.
	World references (geographical or historical)	They laughed and cavorted like competing court jesters.	Like a court jesters joking for the pleasure of a king, the boys laughed and entertained their coach.
	Vocabulary	Their laughter rang out, ostracizing their classmate.	Boys' laughter is hardly ever synthetic, but spontaneous.
	(Add icons for any devices you have covered in class, like figurative devices, rhetorical devices, or grammatical structures.)		

TEXT STRUCTURES: A GROWING COLLECTION

The Story of My Thinking

What I used to think	But this happened	So now I think

A Memory

Where you were	Moment it started	Next moment	Final moment	What you thought

A Colorized Memory

Where you were (dramatized)	Moment it started (dramatized)	Next moment (dramatized)	The final moment (dramatized)	What you thought

Completely Made up Story

Moment involving character(s)	Moment when a problem arises	How the characters try (unsuccessfully) to solve the problem	How the characters solve it (or deal with it)

A Fable

Animals doing something	Conversation between the animals	Action	Result	Moral

Sequel to a Fable

Moral of original fable	But the next day the animals said	And this happened	The result was	New moral

Comparing Notes (Mine and Others)

Some people think . . .	And other people think . . .	But I think . . .	What that tells me . . .

Tevye's Debate

On one hand	On the other hand	But on the other hand	But on the other hand	How I can be guided when the choice is so tough

Evolution of a Term (word or phrase in the prompt)

What the word meant to me when I was 4	What it meant when I was a little older	What the word means to me now	What the word will probably mean when I am ___ (pick an age)

Tribute to the Person Who Taught Me Something

What the lesson is	Flashback to the lesson	Description of the person	Lyrics or words you can remember that person saying (on the subject)	What I wish I could find out now from that person

The Onion – Unlayering What We Know

One (real) belief something we know	How do I know this? (Tell one way, one thing that happened)	If that had not happened, how else would you know it?	If that had not happened, how else would you know it?

Insight Garden/The 11-minute essay

An insight about life	One illustration from literature	One illustration from a movie	An illustration from my life	I wonder

Pet Peeve

What you saw first	What you said to yourself	What else you saw	What you decided	What you know now

I Will Never

I will never . . .	If I did . . .	This would cause . . .	I've seen it before like when . . .	So I have decided that . . .	I will probably change my mind if . . .

Replacement

I need to replace my . . .	I used to . . .	Now it doesn't . . .	A new one would . . .	However . . .	And so . . .

Shopping List

I need to buy . . .	Without it . . .	This would cause . . .	Eventually . . .	And so . . .	I only hope . . .

A time you watched someone else do something on your won't-do list

I don't think I will ever . . .	I don't understand how someone could . . .	It's true that . . .	And so it's so true that . . .	However . . .	So . . .

Prized Possession

I just couldn't do without . . .	It has the most . . .	It has . . .	Before I had it . . .	That's why . . .	Without it, I would . . .

Conversation: One thing you and your friends talk about

When I was young, I wondered about . . .	I thought that probably . . .	Since then . . .	All I really need to know now is . . .	Eventually I'll . . .

Curiosity: One thing you'd like to know about

I have sometimes wondered about . . .	I know that . . .	I also know that . . .	But I can't figure out how . . .	Even so, I will always . . .

Competency: Something you can do well

I've never/always considered myself a . . .	But then . . .	That's when . . .	So now . . .

Conversation: Comparing notes

Some people think . . .	Other people think . . .	I think . . .	What I wonder is . . .

Work Moment (frustrating or satisfying)

Where you were	What you were doing	What you heard/saw	What good (or frustrating) thing happened	What surprised you

Going Against the Grain

Some people think . . .	This seems to happen because . . .	However I believe . . .	But I know people feel strongly . . .	Even so I will always . . .

Contributed by Christi Gonzles

Alternative Solution

Problem	Conventional solution	The problem with that	Another solution

David Brooks Editorials

This happened	An obvious way to think about it is . . .	The problem with that view is . . .	A better way to look at it would be . . .

Contributed by Thomas Newkirk

Giving an Award

Who you choose	One quality they have	One moment where you saw that quality	How that affected you then	What you think of that person still

Contributed by Theresa Phelps

Favorite Activity

I like to _____	My first experience with it	How you do/play it	How it makes you feel	Positive results

Contributed by Theresa Phelps

Ethos

You know (of) this person	You trust this person	This person says _____	It must be true

Pathos

We value these things	Look what happened	Isn't that sad	We must do this _____

Logos

Here is a point	Reason/Evidence	Proven theories	So

Syllogism

If this is true	And this is true	Then this must be true

Cicero's arrangement (dispositio)

Who you are and what you want	Facts of the case	What should be done (your position)	Flaws in opposing arguments	Summary and next steps
Exordium	Narratio	Confirmatio	Refutatio	Peroratio

Curiosity

I have wondered . . .	I figured out that . . .	Then I also figured out . . .	Last I figured out . . .	This all means that . . .	What you can do about it

Robin Pool

Doing Something 101

Truism	Step 1	Step 2	Step 3	Step 4	Results (with image)

Robert Schuler

History of Something

| Why this is | When this happened | What people thought then | What people think now |

Loretta Anderson

Problem/Solution

| Why people deliver messages like this | Our deep belief | How things are supposed to work | The problem | Proof | What we have tried (unsuccessfully) | Our solution |

Declaration of Independence

Dilemma

| Choice: Staying the same or changing | What change would mean | Biggest disadvantage of change | Biggest disadvantage of staying the same | How change might make it worse | What happens if you just don't decide |

Hamlet—Act 3, Scene 1

Now Introducing

| One person's moment using the thing | What problem the thing solves | How the thing works | But one problem the thing creates | Reasons it is a good idea anyway | Data to support the purpose |

From Drive Cam Article

Musing to an object

| Direct address and a question (something you want to know) | Description of one physical chracteristic of the object | Description of another characteristic of the object, with a simile | An imperative to the object; a wish or a hope |

Twinkle, Twinkle, Little Star

TEXT STRUCTURES INVENTED BY KIDS

Hindsight Reflections

This bad situation happened	How I should have reacted	Rather than making the best of a bad situation, how I did react	Now I know

Amanda Grosch

Seeking an Answer

I had this question	I asked somebody for an answer	I asked somebody else to confirm the previous answer	I tested out the answer for myself with this experience	What I learned from my experience

Giovanni Ocasio

Deception

I saw this happen	And so I did this	But then I realized	So now I know

Destiny Costly

We Agreed

I said this	And she/he said that	But we both agree on this

Eric Flores

The Right Choice

My problem	What my friend thinks I should do	So I decided to . . .	Now I think

Rebecca Dschuden

Why We Do Things

This event happened	It caused me to be in this mood	Which caused this to happen	So now I know

Shawn St. Hilaire

Wishful Thinking

One problem in the world	Why it is this way	What you wish it would be like

Gisela Navarro

Maturing Thoughts (over a key word in the prompt)

How important it was to you when you were _____ (young)	How important it was to you when you were _____ (older)	How important it is to you now	How your thoughts changed as you grew older

Marissa LaRochelle

The Unexpected Reaction

What I said	How the listener reacted	What I learned

Samantha Runnels

Action Up

I used to act like this	Then I went through this	Which made me consider the future like this	So now I act like this

Casey Towle

Explanation of a Term

| Dictionary-like definition | Your personal definition | What feeling you get from it | What others make you think | Example in society today | Anther example (optional) |

Cary Inzerello

Following a Path

| Where I started out in life | Where I found myself | Where I am now | Where I might be in the future |

Rebekah Long

A Box of Chocolates

| What happened | What you expected to get | What you really got | How you reacted |

Marco Vidarri

Influences and Consequences

| I was taught this | But I was influenced by this | So I did this | And the consequences were this |

Adam Saenz

A Bad Choice

| A choice you made | What happened after that choice | Things you learned later about that choice | What you think now about that choice you made |

Joseph Kidder

Never Ever

What I've never done	Why I've never done it	Will I ever do it?

Adrian Martinez

Temptations

How someone else was tempted	So I was tempted	So then we did this	Then this happened	Then this happened

Tabitha Flores

True Friends

My friend would always do this	So I believe this about them	Then over time, they started/stopped doing this	So now I think this about them

Dash Dalrymple

Anxiety

A fear I have . . .	What made me scared . . .	Will I be scared in the future?

Amanda Garza

Change of Heart

Because I thought this . . .	I used to feel this . . .	But this happened . . .	So now I feel this . . .	Which makes me think that . . .

Anissa Castaña

Discovering the Fireworks

What the spectacular event was	How it made you feel	Why it made you feel that way	What it made you realize

Wrong Assumption

I made this wrong assumption	Something happened as a consequence	I learned the truth	So now I believe

Diana Diaz

Garden of Eden

One time long ago	As time passed	Now . . .

Tara Coleman

Expert Testimony

According to this person	According to this other person . . .	But according to me . . .	So now I think . . .

LaQuette Barksdale

Alternate Choices

I can either do this . . .	Or I can do this	I choose _____ because

Marisa Farias

May be photocopied for classroom use. © 2012 Gretchen S. Bernabei and Dorothy Hall from *The Story of My Thinking* (Heinemann: Portsmouth, NH).

Elimination or Confirmation

I've never been sure if	But I've always suspected	Because once I experienced	Which made me think that	And finally I realized

Michael Gonzalez

Sensory Associations

When I heard/ smell/see . . .	It reminds me of . . .	Which makes me feel . . .	Because . . .

Julee Lanum

The Evolution of a Habit

I used to have this habit	Because I thought this	But then this happened	As a result, the habit was _____

Alexander Burke

The Real Deal

I saw someone	I assumed . . .	When actually . . .	So now I understand . . .

Amber Wojtek

What is it? (Defining a Word)

Is it this?	Or this?	Or this?	A memory	Which makes me realize it's this

Adrian Martinez

May be photocopied for classroom use. © 2012 Gretchen S. Bernabei and Dorothy Hall from *The Story of My Thinking* (Heinemann: Portsmouth, NH).

Confusing Testimony

| Someone told me (an inaccurate thing) | Then I checked I with someone else | And that person set me straight | How I explain that 1st person's misinformation |

Alexander Burke

Yellow Brick Road

| This (bad thing) happened | And this is how I reacted | Then later something similar happened | So, reflecting on my prior experience, this time I did this instead |

Nathan McCann

Find and Truth Through Experience

| I heard this | But I thought the opposite | Then I had this experience | Now I think this |

Nathan Hay

Not on my Nerves Any More

| I used to hate it when other people . . . | But then I realized I also did it | So now when I see other people doing it I remember that . . . |

Tricia Asher

Crossing the River Again

| A recurring challenge | How the challenge first came up | But since then this happened | How I now meet the challenge | How it still challenges me |

Clayton Graham

Use Your Noodle

I was taught this	What I thought about what I was taught	But this happened	So what I now think about what I was taught

Brianna Cook

You Never Know

I assumed . . .	But it turned out . . .	So now I think . . .

Matt Cadena

The Idea

I think about a . . .	I ask other people what they think	We put our thoughts together	We came up with a final decision

Leanna Hernandez

Day Dreamer

Sometimes I'm thinking a lot about	What made me think it	What this thought means

Sarah Crickmore

With This in Mind

One true thing	With this in mind, it will not be possible for _____	One hardship that will create	So now I wonder

Ashley Brzostowski

The Game

There was a perfect time when . . .	But then . . .	Now I know . . .

Stacey Arias

Making a Change

One thing I wanted to change	What was stopping me	Even thought I know this . . .	So . . .

Samantha Ross

Thinking Hurts

This happened	Which caused this	Which made this happen	Which caused this	Which made me think this

Stephen Crisp

Faith in Spite of Experience

Despite this repeated bad thing happening . . .	I know that . . .	So I will do this

Carmen Garcia

Wisdom Tug-of-War

I was always told to . . .	Then I actually wanted	In order to keep me on the right path	But instead I	I slowly realized that

Bernard Gottschalk

Your Actions

Something makes you too confident in this belief	Your actions cause a downfall	So now, you act like this	Because now you believe

Marcus Garcia

Deciding Through Diverse Opinions

We did this	I thought it was a bad idea because	But others thought differently	So together we concluded	So we did this

Megan Morefield

Changing Gears

_____ is (characteristic)	One thing they did that shows this	When asked why he/she behaved in this manner	Gradually	To this day . . .

Inspired by Elise Leal

Wo . . . Wo . . . Wonder

I used to wonder	Because	But then this happened	So I no longer wonder; now I think . . .

Re'Shelle Kibler

Line of Thought

One time this happened	Which made this happen	Which made me realize this	So this happened

Chris Clay

Seeing is Believing

What I did first	But then I saw	And that made me think	So then I did this . . .

Molly Pierce and Sarah Sinclair

She Saw

She saw . . .	And she thought	I saw the same thing	And I thought	So I guess

Adria Warner

Who Reacted When

Why this happened	How this happened	When this happened	What people thought about it

Alex Blue

Metamorphosis

How you felt before it happened	How you felt while it was happening	How you felt after it happened	How you feel now	What you believe now

Kelsey Mahan

What the Heck

My friends did this	I thought about it	I believe _____ so	I did this	They reacted like this	So now, we . . .

Casey Lewis

The Influence of We

What I thought	How I felt about this thought	What others thought about my thoughts	What I thought about my thoughts after others told me what they thought	What I know

Sarah Chu

Cause and Effect

I did this	It caused this	Now I know this

Celeste Ramirez

Life Lesson, Past and Future

What the life lesson is	What it means to you	How it affected your life (past)	How it will affect your life (future)

Adam Hinds

Backfire

I did this	Because of _____	What I was hoping for	But instead this happened	So now I think

Armando Barrera

Life Lessons Learned

I never realized _____	Until this happened	Then I realized	So now I try . . .

Amanda Walker

Discovering a Lie

Someone told me	So I believed	Then I found out	So now I think/know

Alyssa Flores

Changing Your Mind

I believe this	But society proved me wrong by doing this	So then I believe this	But then this happened	So now I believe this

Greg Herbst

I Wish

I wish that	But I know	And knowing this	Makes me believe . . .

Steven Young

Arguing

I said this . . .	They said that . . .	We argued because of _____	How we resolve it	Now I think this

Remy Locasio

Then What?

One way I got in trouble	After that this happened	Then this happened	I was thinking about my consequences	So now I think

Artemis Martinez and Justin Garza

Name: _____

Planning Sheet

Type of Writing (Check One)

☐ Writing about myself   ☐ Writing to inform me   ☐ Writing to inform others   ☐ Writing to persuade   ☐ Writing about literature

Put your **truism** (aka assertion aka problem aka main question) here.

_____

_____

Put your **text structure** here.

☐ ☐ ☐ ☐ ☐ ☐

Write your **kernel essay** here.

1. _____

2. _____

3. _____

4. _____

5. _____

6. _____

Plan for **details**:

ACTION DETAIL		INFOSHOTS	
☐ snapshots	☐ sensory details	☐ description	☐ synonyms/antonyms
☐ thoughtshots	☐ ba-da-bing	☐ compare/contrast	☐ part/whole
☐ dialogue	☐ _____	☐ cause/effect	☐ item/category
		☐ before/after	☐ _____

Name: _____

Elastic Kernel

Your Topic: _____

How could you write about this topic in different ways?

NARRATIVE (What Happened)	EXPOSITORY (What Hapened)	ARGUMENTATION (What Should Happen)
Memory driven: what happened in your life, and what did it mean to you?	**Curiosity driven:** what would other people want to know? What else would you want to find out?	**Driven by the need for change:** right/wrong, good/better, current ways/better ways
Ex: The moment that we caught a marlin	**All about** fishing tackle How to catch a marlin **Different kinds** of fishing trips **Background on** catch-and-release **Tips for** safe fishing	**Why** catch-and-release is important **Why** families **should** fish together **Why** gulf waters **should** be protected The value of male bonding over fishing **The benefits of** spending time with your family out in nature

Titles That Sell Informational Articles

All About _____ and Why It Matters

Everything You Need to Know About _____

What You Never Knew About _____

Top Ten Reasons for _____

The Secret(s) Behind _____

The Truth About _____

Amazing Facts About _____

The Real Story About _____

The _____ Controversy

Your Personal Guide to _____

Success with _____

Win Big with _____

Prizewinning _____

The Ultimate Scoop on _____

Hidden Secrets About _____

An Essential Guide to _____

The Zen of _____

_____ for Dummies

Lessons from a _____

Just Say No to _____

Little Known Facts About

The Secret Life of _____

Infoshots

REQUIREMENT/ACTION

Money is required to buy a gift.

___ is required in order to ___.

MARY VARGAS

User/Tool

A worker uses a shovel.

___ uses ___.

Marielle Holdsworth | Ethan Hays

OPPOSITES

Day is the opposite of night.

___ is the opposite of ___.

G. Bernabei

SYNONYMS (SAME)

this mug is almost the same as that mug.

___ is almost the same as ___.

Sydney Lotz

DEFINING CHARACTERISTIC

A sheep can be described as soft. Pillow

___ can be described as ___.

G. Bernabei

PART/WHOLE

A kernel is part of an ear.

A ___ is part of a ___.

Bree Taha

CAUSE / EFFECT

A cactus can cause the need for a bandaid.

___ can cause ___.

Angelica Blake

OBJECT/FUNCTION

A violin is used for creating music.

___ is used for ___.

Marina Mares

Infoshots

(TRANSFORMATION)
BEFORE/AFTER

A cow can be transformed into hamburger.

___ transforms into ___.

MARINA MARES

ITEM /CATEGORY

A banana is a type of fruit.

___ is a type of ___.

JACOB GUTIERREZ

TYPICAL LOCATION

McDonald's French Fries are located at McDonald's.

___ is usually located ___.
(what)   (where)

marina mares | Alex Cisneros

Extreme Degrees

The large lego block is a large version of the small lego block.

___ is a _different_ version of ___.

Marina Mares

Item / Ingredient

Sweet Peas   Mixed vegetables

Peas are an ingredient in mixed vegetables.

___ is an ingredient in ___.

alejandro Braun

Tool / Product

typewriter   BOOK

A typewriter is used to create a book.

A ___ is used to create ___.

Julie Hernendez | Gabrielle Hutchinson

Object / Use

cup   Cocoa Cola

A cup is used to hold a drink.

___ is used for ___

Ryan Richardson

Journal Hunt

Look through your journal; find entries. List phrases and page numbers.

W A S	W A I	W + D
Best moments	Things You Explained (Even a Little)	Things You'd Like to Change
1.	1.	1.
2.	2.	2.
3.	3.	3.
4.	4.	4.
Worst moments	5.	5.
1.	6.	Things (Almost) Everyone Agrees About
2.	Things You Were (Are) Curious About	1.
3.	1.	2.
Moments of Confusion	2.	3.
1.	3.	4.
2.	4.	5.
3.	5.	Things You Need(ed)
Things You Believe(d)	6.	1.
1.	Things You Need (ed) to Find Out About	2.
2.	1.	3
3.	2.	4.
Changes You See In You	3.	5.
1.	4.	Things You Need Other People to Do
2.	5.	1.
3.	Things You Can Do	2.
Changes In How You See Others/the World	1.	3.
1.	2.	4.
2.	3.	5.
3.	4.	

Bank of Expository Prompts

In each of the following, the word *explain* signals an expository (not narrative) essay. You could change any of the content words in the prompts, especially the adjectives, to create many more prompts.

Who is the most surprising person you know? Write an essay about that person, explaining what makes him or her so surprising.

Who is the most helpful person you know? Write an essay about that person, explaining what makes him or her so helpful.

Who is the most focused person you know? Write an essay about that person, explaining what makes him or her so focused.

Who is the funniest person you know? Write an essay about that person, explaining what makes him or her so funny.

Where is the place you consider the most exciting? Write an essay about that place, explaining what makes it so exciting.

Where is a place you consider the most peaceful? Write an essay about that place, explaining what makes it so peaceful.

What is an important possession you have lost? Write an essay about that possession, explaining its importance to you.

What is one of your favorite possessions? Write an essay about that possession, explaining what makes it one of your favorites.

Explain the meaning of *bravery*.

Explain the importance of failure.

Explain the significance of responsibility.

Explain the effects of stress.

Explain the kinds of friendship.

Explain the value of hope.

Explain the sources of pride.

Explain the difficulties of trustworthiness.

Name: _____

Checking Your Essay

ORGANIZATION AND STRUCTURE	One paragraph for each kernel sentence?	Is your planning sheet attached? (text structure boxes and kernel essay)	**8 points**	
DEPTH	2 or more 3-in-1 infoshots?	Highlight yellow	**8 points**	
	2 snapshots?	Highlight blue	**4 points**	
WORD CHOICE	3 or more vocabulary words?	Underline these	**4 points**	
MECHANICS	Periods? Proper nouns capitalized? Apostrophes correct?		**4 points**	
PROOFREADING	3 "I heard this" signatures?	Did you listen as you read?	**2 points**	
FORMAT	Is your heading on the top left?	Title centered, capitalized, and not underlined?		

Total: 30 points

Build an Opinion Prompt

Explain why I	(choose one)	(choose one)
	☐ crave	☐ times
	☐ need	☐ things—possessions
	☐ enjoy	☐ activities
	☐ like	☐ places
	☐ dislike	☐ abstract concepts
	☐ detest	
	☐ abhor	

TIMES	POSSESSIONS	ACTIVITIES	PLACES	ABSTRACT CONCEPTS
1898 (or another year)	awards	apologizing	airport	acceptance
afternoon	basketball	biking	backyard	bravery
birthdays	cameras	cooking	beach	caring
breakfast	candy	crying	beauty shop	confusion
early morning	chocolate	dreaming	bookstore	disappointment
far into the future	electronics	exercising	car	embarrassment
last semester	food	falling	college	envy
last week	furniture	gossiping	country	excitement
last year	glasses	hopping	dollhouse	failure
naptime	gym bag	interrupting	ecosystems	fear
nighttime	jewelry	jumping	front seat	freedom
noon	junk	laughing	gardens	friendship
now	library books	painting	gas station	frustration
party time	money	planning	grocery store	happiness
study time	movies	pondering	highway	honor
summertime	pets	reading	islands	hope
sunrise	plants	running	Jacuzzi	independence
sunset	rugs	sewing	land	loneliness
today	school supplies	shopping	library	love
tomorrow	shoes	singing	mine shaft	loyalty
Tuesday	skates	skating	mountains	patriotism
when i was younger	towel	sleeping	movie theatre	pride
winter	toys	smiling	north	respect
years ago	trash can	spying	ocean	responsibility
yesterday		swimming	park	stress
		talking	place of worship	trustworthiness
		texting	pool	worry
		thinking	rain forest	
		washing hands	rooms	
		watching movies/TV	seashore	
		whispering	sports arena	
		wishing	tree house	
		writing	underwater	

① Topic of interest: _____

② Nickname of Structure: _____

[ ] → [ ] → [ ] → [ ] → [ ] → [ ]

④ Questions from Listeners

③ Kernel Essay

1. _____
2. _____
3. _____
4. _____
5. _____
6. _____

⑤ infoshots = template sentence + jerktalk

Sticky notes here

SIGNATURES OF LISTENERS
1.
2.
3.

⑥ Design: Lay out your structure and plan for where to embed your infoshots

Three-in-One Infoshots: Try It!

Write sentences using the template patterns. Then combine them to create "sneaky infoshots."

Three	French toast is the opposite of hamburgers.
One	French toast can be described as amazingness.
	French toast changes lives!
	As opposed to a hamburger, the amazing French toast can definitely change your life.
	—Batya K., grade 8

Try it!

Three	1. _____ _____ _____ 2. _____ _____ _____ 3. _____ _____ _____

One	

Name: _____

Self-Selected Reading Book Essay Assignment and Pre-Writing

What is the best thing about your book? _____

Title of book: _____

Author: _____

Plot summary: _____

_____

_____

Choose a **text structure** to talk about your book. Then write a **kernel essay** about one aspect of the book. Turn this page in for a maximum grade of B. If you would like a grade of A, then flesh out your kernel essay with details from the book, and turn in that essay with this page. The final essay should range from 400 to 700 words, typed.

Name of structure: _____

Kernel essay:

1. _____

2. _____

3. _____

4. _____

5. _____

6. _____

Heard by: (three signatures) _____

_____

Name: _____

Science Fair Project Abstract

Put your **title here**

_____
_____
_____

Text structure: **Science Fair Abstract**

what question you are answering (your problem)	what you suspected was true (your hypothesis)	what you did (your steps, or experiment procedure)	what happened (your results)	what that means (your conclusion)	

Write your **kernel essay** here.

1. _____

2. _____

3. _____

4. _____

5. _____

6. _____

Create your **abstract** like this

Paragraph 1: sentences 1 and 2.

Paragraph 2: your steps.

Paragraph 3: sentences 4 and 5.

WORKS CITED

Aristotle, and Lane Cooper. 1932. *The Rhetoric of Aristotle, an Expanded Translation with Supplementary Examples for Students of Composition and Public Speaking.* New York: D. Appleton.

Bernabei, Gretchen. 2005. *Reviving the Essay.* Shoreham, VT: Discover Writing Press.

Bernabei, Gretchen. 2010. *Lightning in a Bottle: Visual Prompts and Insights.* DVD. San Antonio, TX: Trail of Breadcrumbs.

Brock, Paula. 2002. *Nudges: Thinking, Writing, Vocabulary, and Spelling.* Spring, TX: Absey & Company.

Bruner, J. S. 1986. *Actual Minds. Possible Worlds.* Cambridge, MA: Harvard University Press.

Council of Writing Program Administrators, National Council of Teachers of English, and National Writing Project. 2011. *Framework for Success in Postsecondary Writing.* Rep. Creative Commons.

Cowan, Elizabeth. 1980. *Writing.* Hoboken, NJ: Wiley.

Daniels, Harvey. 2002. "Expository Text in Literature Circles." *Voices from the Middle* 9.4: 7–14.

Daniels, Harvey, and Nancy Steineke. 2011. *Texts and Lessons for Content-Area Reading.* Portsmouth, NH: Heinemann.

Erasmus, Desiderius, Craig R. Thompson, Betty I. Knott, Brian McGregor, and Desiderius Erasmus. *De Copia; De Ratione Studii.* 1978. Toronto: University of Toronto.

Graff, Gerald, and Cathy Birkenstein. 2007. *"They Say/I Say": The Moves That Matter in Persuasive Writing.* New York: W.W. Norton.

Killgallon, Don, and Jenny Killgallon. 2000. *Sentence Composing for Elementary School: A Workbook to Build Better Sentences.* Portsmouth, NH: Heinemann.

Kinneavy, James L. 1971. *A Theory of Discourse.* Englewood Cliffs, NJ: Prentice-Hall.

Lane, Barry, and Gretchen Bernabei. 2001. *Why We Must Run with Scissors: Voice Lessons in Persuasive Writing.* Shoreham, VT: Discover Writing Press.

Miller, Carol Rawlings. 2008. Foreword by Jim Burke. *Strange Bedfellows: Surprising Text Pairs and Lessons for Reading and Writing across Genres.* Portsmouth, NH: Heinemann.

Moffett, James. 1968. *Teaching the Universe of Discourse.* Boston: Houghton Mifflin.

Neeld, Elizabeth Cowan, and Gregory Cowan. 1986. *Writing.* Glenview, IL: Scott, Foresman.

Newkirk, Thomas. 2009. *Holding On to Good Ideas in a Time of Bad Ones: Six Literacy Principles Worth Fighting For.* Portsmouth, NH: Heinemann.

———. 2005.*The School Essay Manifesto: Reclaiming the Essay for Students and Teachers.* Shoreham, VT: Discover Writing Press.

Romano, Tom. 2000. *Blending Genre, Altering Style: Writing Multigenre Papers.* Portsmouth, NH: Heinemann.